D0708048

BOWLER, Peter

The superior person's third
book of words

THE SUPERIOR PERSON'S
THIRD
BOOK OF WORDS

THE SUPERIOR PERSON'S
THIRD
BOOK OF WORDS

PETER BOWLER

BLOOMSBURY

First published in Great Britain 2004

First US edition published in 2001 by
David R. Godine, Publisher, Inc.,
Post Office Box 450, Jaffrey, New Hampshire 03452

Published by arrangement with David R. Godine, Publisher, Inc.,
9 Hamilton Place, Boston, Massachusetts 02108

Bloomsbury Publishing Plc, 38 Soho Square, London W1D 3HB

A CIP catalogue record for this book is available from the
British Library.

ISBN 0 7475 6918 5

10 9 8 7 6 5 4 3 2 1

Designed by Nathan Burton
Typeset by Dorchester Typesetting Group Ltd
Printed by Clays Ltd, St Ives plc

All papers used by Bloomsbury Publishing are natural, recyclable
products made from wood grown in well-managed forests. The
manufacturing processes conform to the environmental
regulations of the country of origin.

For Diane, with love

Proem (q.v.)

Several years ago, I was asked to write a sequel to my first book, the infamous *Superior Person's Book of Words*. The result was *The Superior Person's Second Book of Words*.

The rest is history. The tacit acclaim of the illuminati, the unaccountable silence of major literary awards the world over, the fan mail from mentally disturbed lexicographers manqué on the Indian subcontinent ... Now, of course, both books are accepted as classics of their kind. In those universities where the age-old skills of reading and writing are still remembered, students may be found poring over their tattered Bowlerian volumes in secret, as they crouch behind ancient stone walls to avoid their compulsory classes in Corporate Team Membership Skills. Overnight, the same chalked message appears on city walls everywhere: Verbarian Ultracrepidarianism Lives!

'Words should not be policed,' said the kalokagathical Camille Paglia, and readers are assured that the many ideologically incorrect prejudices of the author, so liberally displayed in the first two volumes, appear also in the present one, as a positive incentive to the nation's militant puritans to learn to read.

For those new to the genre, may I briefly restate my purpose: to equip the person in the street with new and better verbal weapons. Words that are real and may be found in dictionaries but which have too long lain there unseen and forgotten. Words that may give the reader, so to speak, a more finely machined engine for the language that they speak, so that they may the more readily assert a fitting ascendancy over their fellows at the traffic lights of life.

My illustrative examples of the use of the words in sentences sometimes involve the names of people. Be it clearly understood that these are invented names, and do not constitute a pathetic attempt on my part to score off my friends and relatives. However, the snippets of instructive factual information, including anecdotes of historical figures such as Porson, Babbage and Galton, are, hard as this may be to believe, absolutely true. Similarly, with the exception of a mere two or three neoterisms (q.v.), all the words contained herein are real words which have been found in authoritative sources. In the odd half-dozen cases where an explanatory passage in a definition itself contains an unfamiliar word, and that word cannot be found defined herein, it will be found defined in one of the two previous *Words* books, or in any good dictionary.

My principal sources are those listed on page 145; but I have also found many curious and sometimes astonishing items in such other works as the excellent *Fontana Dictionary of Modern Thought*, Mackay's *Extraordinary Popular Delusions and the Madness of Crowds*, Rawcliffe's *Illusions and Delusions of the Supernatural and the Occult*, the bloodcurdling *Anomalies and Curiosities of Medicine* by Gould and Pyle, Halliwell's *Dictionary of Archaic Words*, Deutch's *The Australian Magician's Handbook*, the *Simple Church Dictionary* of 'A.S.', Mollett's *Dictionary of Art and Archaeology*, Slonimsky's *Lexicon of Musical Invective* and Cuddon's *Dictionary of Literary Terms*.

I thank my wife for putting up with someone who

reads dictionaries in bed, from time to time uttering little cries of delight and saying 'Listen to this one!' when she is trying to get to sleep. Also those who have encouraged me to persist with these lexicographical *jeux d'esprits*, including Professor John Pearn, to whom I owe the happy concept of 'Figure of Speech of the Month' (see under *trope*).

It is now time for me to lay before you, once again, my verbarian exotica. As always, I have included one or two deliberate mistakes, in the hope of keeping you awake. Do not write to me about these.

Peter Bowler, 2001

A

AASVOGEL *n.* A vulture. Ideal term for oral insults, the sound being even more offensive than the meaning, which no-one will know anyway.

ABA *n.* A sleeveless garment of camel or goat hair, worn in the Middle East. Pronounced 'arbour', and therefore useless for laboured Abba puns, but a nicely confusing name for your husband's tank tops, or, as such garments are sometimes risibly called, 'muscle tops'.

ABACISCUS *n.* A square tile in a mosaic floor. 'Ooh,' you exclaim with a wince, on entering your host's palatial foyer, 'I think I've just trodden on an abaciscus!'

ABJURATION *n.* The act of renouncing, forswearing or repudiating. 'At what part of the service does the abjuration take place?' you innocently ask the vicar during his little talk with you and your fiancée about the forthcoming wedding ceremony.

ACMEISM *n.* A movement against symbolism and in favour of lucidity and definiteness in poetry, begun in Russia in 1910. 'Don't talk to me about the ineffable lightness of being, Jarrod, just because you want to go to this overnight party. I'm an acmeist, remember. Just tell me: will there or will there not be adult supervision?'

ACORPORAL *a.* Without a body. In response to a remark by Samuel Rogers that in moments of extreme danger it was very desirable to have presence of mind, the Reverend Sydney Smith replied that he would rather have absence of body. This was said on the very same night that Smith, dining at Rogers' home, was asked for his opinion of a new lighting system installed by Rogers in the dining room, in such a way that the light was directed at the ceiling, leaving the table below in subdued lighting. Smith replied that he did not like the new system at all, 'for all is light above, and all below is darkness and gnashing of teeth'.

acorporal

ACQUITMENT *n.* You think this is an accounting term, but more importantly it is a word used by stage and close-up magicians. For them, an acquitment is a series of moves designed to convince the audience that both the magician's hands are empty. The essence of the acquitment is that an object is secretly passed from hand to hand, one hand and then the other being shown to be empty. 'I know you don't like me associating with Leroy, Mom, just because he works at the racetrack; but I'm learning a lot from him. Today he showed me all about acquitments.'

ACROAMA *n.* A dramatic recitation during a meal; a lecture to the initiated. 'Mother, I have agreed to sit down at the dinner table and not to eat my food with my fingers. Is that not enough? Must I submit to acroama as well?'

ADJURATION *n.* A formula used in the conjuring of evil spirits, in order to compel them to do or say what ever you demand. Unfortunately there is no formula for compelling members of the opposite sex to do or say whatever you demand. You could try it on, of course. 'I adjure you, Melissa, to …'; but if the maiden merely says, 'What did you say?' you could always claim that the word you used was 'implore'.

AGITOPHASIA *n.* A hysterical condition causing extreme rapidity of speech. 'Nix on the agitophasia, Maurice; the quickness of the hand may deceive the eye, but not the voice the mind. Your excuses are pathetic. You will return to the school hall, and you will take part in the pantomime, and you will sing along with little Deirdre in the feature spot in the finale, dressed as the Fairy King, whether you like it or not. Your mother has spoken.'

AICHMOPHOBIA *n.* Extreme fear of the sight of any sharp-pointed instrument, whether a needle, a nail, a thorn, a spike, etc. James I of England suffered from this phobia, and could not endure the appearance of a drawn sword.

ALGOPHOBIA *n.* The morbid dread of pain. As a warning to those who have been lulled into a false sense of security at the dentist's by the latter's more or less routine use of local anaesthetics, the author, a true algophobe, relates this cautionary tale of his encounter with a London dentist. 'It's just a little one,' said the dentist, in the most casual and reassuring tone, 'do you want to bother with an anaesthetic this time?' 'No,' I manfully replied. In an instant the drill was in my mouth, and through a curtain of unendurable pain I heard the dentist say, 'Suit yourself; it won't hurt me!' Like all algophobes, I have never been able to transcend dental medication. Hmmm ... perhaps if you said it aloud ...

ALLOPATHY *n.* Conventional medical treatment, as opposed to so-called 'alternative' medicines such as homoeopathy, reflexology, etc. If your New Age cousin is persistently refusing to see the doctor about her condition, you could perhaps convince her to do so by secretively whispering to her: 'You know, of course, that he's an allopath?'

ALPHITOMANCY *n.* A method of determing the guilt or innocence of a person by feeding him a barley loaf. If indigestion ensues, the person is guilty. Some may say that if indigestion ensues after eating anything at all prepared by their best beloved, they are held by the latter to be guilty.

AMBIVIUM *n.* Any street or road leading *around* a place rather than to it. The route that you and I invariably take.

AMPLEXUS *n.* Sexual intercourse between amphibians such as frogs or toads, in which an embrace occurs but the eggs are fertilised externally. (An *amplexation* is an embrace, whether between frogs or anyone.) 'So this is your first scuba lesson, Miss Pomfrey? Well, first, we'll familiarise ourselves with the equipment, have some trial shallow-water dives, and finish off the day with the amplexus.'

AMPYX *n.* A general term to denote any net made of string, bands or ribbons, forming a head-dress. Also, happily, the ornamental strips of leather that fulfil a similar purpose for a horse. Your great-aunt's hairnet could be so characterised.

ANDROPHOBIA *n.* The morbid dread of men. The existence of the term implies that somewhere, at some time, there must be someone with a morbid dread of me. I find this distinctly empowering, and would very much like to meet this person.

ARRESTING GEAR *phr.* The device on an aircraft carrier which abruptly stops the forward movement of a landing aeroplane. The Superior Person's term for the handbrake of a car.

ASRAH ILLUSION *n.* Name of a well-known stage illusion in which a woman is levitated while reclining under a large cloth, which is suddenly whisked away to show that she has vanished.

'Desirée, if you really want to appear in my Asrah Illusion, you realise, don't you, that we will need to practise down in the basement for quite a few weeks? In absolute secrecy? Oh, did I mention that it's vital to the levitation effect that you be naked? But don't worry, you'll be entirely covered with a cloth for virtually the entire act.'

astasia-abasia

ASTASIA-ABASIA *n.* A functional inability to stand or walk despite the fact that the patient retains good muscular co-ordination while lying in bed, especially in the handling of the drinks tray and the TV remote. See also *basophobia*.

ASTEISM *n.* An ingeniously polite insult. In some regards, this book may be regarded as an asteisticon.

ASTROLOGY *n.* Pathetic body of so-called learning which professes to predict the future and reveal the influence of the heavenly bodies on the affairs of men. If men want to influence the affairs of heavenly bodies, the recommended procedure is to buy *two* copies of the coming year's astrology guide, give one to the lady whose heavenly body you aspire to, *and secretly keep the other copy yourself*. In this way, you will know in advance what your lady expects or hopes for from day to day, and will be ideally placed to take due advantage of this knowledge. You don't get this sort of information in other dictionaries.

ASTROPHOBIA, OR **ASTROPAPHOBIA** *n.* The morbid dread of being struck by lightning, and hence the fear of thunder and storms generally. The Emperors Augustus and Caligula were sufferers from this phobia. 'Open the windows wide, my children, and let your mother rejoice in the storm in all its fury! Give her astrophobia free reign!'

ATTORNMENT *n.* A formal procedure from the feudal age in which a tenant acknowledges the authority of a new lord. 'Here is the engagement ring, oh my dearest; and here the affidavit of attornment for your signature ...'

AUTODEFENESTRATION *n.* The act of throwing oneself out of a window. Illustrated by the true case of Mrs Vera Czermak, who discovered that her husband was being unfaithful to her and attempted to end her life by jumping out of the window of her third-floor flat in Prague. At the moment she jumped, her husband happened to walk by beneath the window. She landed on top of him, and survived. He died.

AUTOPHOBIA *n.* Not, as might be imagined, the fear of automobiles, but the morbid dread of oneself, or of being alone. Do vampires, perhaps, have autophobia? They ought to. Politicians, perhaps?

7

AUTOTOMY *n.* The spontaneous shedding by a living organism of part of itself, as for example in the case of crabs and salamanders. 'I don't mind cleaning the house, mother, but I will *not* clean Justin's room! It's autotomy hell in there! There are so many of his hairs and skin cells all over the carpet that the slightest movement creates an organic dust storm!'

AVERRING *n.* Begging by a boy in the nude to arouse sympathy. 'Er – I wonder, Mrs Armitage, if tonight, while Mr Armitage is out, I might try out my averring, if you wouldn't mind being my audience?'

AVICULARIUM *n.* A prehensile organ, not unlike a beak, in certain small aquatic creatures. 'If you're going to stay out in the sun, Lachlan, wear something on your avicularium!'

AXILLA *n.* The armpit. References to axillary emanations would seem to be the go with this one.

AZOTH *n.* Mercury; the name given by alchemists to the universal remedy of Paracelsus. 'How stands the azoth this day?' you robustly enquire, on seeing a colleague peering at the wall thermometer.

autophobia

B

BARBITURATE *n.* A well-known class of narcotic pharmaceutical, as you well know. But did you know that it is named after a Munich waitress named Barbara, who helped its discoverer, Nobel Prize winner Johann Bäyer (1835–1917), in his work by supplying him with her entire urinary output, nicely bottled, over an extended period of time, so that he would have the necessary large quantities of urea needed for his work? For that matter, did you *want* to know that?

BASOPHOBIA *n.* A hysterical fear of falling which is so overwhelming that it effectively prevents the sufferer from even attempting to stand or walk. In *ananastasia*, the sufferer is unable to raise himself from a recumbent to a sitting position; and *acathisia* prevents the sufferer from remaining in a sitting position. Then there's also *astasia-abasia* (q.v.). All of these are good for deferments of exams on medical grounds, exemption from military service, excusal from jury duty, etc.

BATHOPHOBIA *n.* The morbid dread, not of baths, as one might expect, but of depth. Use the term in a metaphorical sense: 'Jeremy's not enrolling in Differential Calculus I after all, this year. Typical! He always was a bathophobe.'

BAYADERE *n.* Two distinct meanings. A dancing girl; and a fabric with crosswise stripes (the kind fat people are not supposed to wear). 'It's kind of you to be so hospitable, Madgwick! Delighted to accept your suggestion that you show me what the town has to offer. Since you ask my preferences, I wonder what the chances would be of a little bayadere for the night?'

BETAKE *v.* An archaic verb, entirely appropriate for Superior Person use. To take (yourself) to something or somewhere. To go. Like 'hie', used reflexively. 'Given the weather, I betook myself to the cinema today; after which I did hie me to the pizza palace.'

BISULCATE *a.* Cloven-hoofed. 'I don't know about Bastian being the devil, but given those shoes he wears I wouldn't be at all surprised to find that he was bisulcate.'

BIVALENCE *n.* The principle that every sentence is either true or false. Including that one. 'But, darling, I swear that every single thing I say is absolutely bivalent.'

BLUNGER *n.* A wooden implement rather like an oversize spatula, used in the manufacture of ceramics when mixing clay and water. Used in this sense, a boring word. But as a term of meaningless abuse ... much more satisfying. The *g*, by the way, is pronounced as a *j*. (See *bogtrotter*.)

BLUNTIE *n.* A Scottish term for a dunce or dunderhead. For reasons unknown to the author, there are many other Scottish terms with a similar significance.

BOGTROTTER *n.* One who trots across, and by implication lives among, bogs. 'Sir, you are nothing but a blunger and a bogtrotter!'

BOHORDAMENTUM *n.* In medieval times, a jousting match with mock lances. The modern equivalent is your children's play with toy *Star Wars* light sabres. 'If you kids must career all round the back yard with those sabre things, just remember we don't have bohordamentum insurance!'

BOVID *n.* A member of the Bovidae family, i.e., ruminant animals such as sheep, cattle and goats with a pair of non-deciduous, non-branching horns. In the unlikely event of your being approached by a gum-chewing Mephistopheles offering a deal of some kind, you could begin by adopting a superior attitude with a remark along the lines of your not doing business with a mere bovid. (You might as well score at least one point off him; we both know he's going to win you over in the end.)

BOWDLERISE *v.* To edit a text with prudish intent, expurgating unseemly passages. After Dr Thomas Bowdler's 1818 *Family Edition of the Works of Shakespeare*. In fact, history has been quite unfair in branding Bowdler as a puritanical wowser, since a reading of his edition by your intrepid author revealed that his 'bowdlerisation' consisted almost exclusively of the replacement of a few select words such as 'whore' while retaining all the lovely violence and sex. See for example his *Titus Andronicus*, in which, I assure you, none of the rape and dismemberment is left to the imagination. A better example of what most of us wrongly think of as Bowdlerisation is the editorial work of the Reverend James Plumptre, a contemporary of Bowdler who *did* amend famous poetry from a strictly moralistic standpoint, often adding whole lines and stanzas of his own. In 'Hark! hark! the lark' from *Cymbeline*, he takes Shakespeare's lines 'With everything that pretty is / My lady sweet, arise' and changes them to 'With everything that pretty is / For shame, thou sluggard, rise'. It is not widely known, by the way, that A. W. Verity, an editor of school editions of Shakespeare recent enough to have been used in my own time, cut out passages which he thought indecent.

BRACHIATE *v.* To swing through the air as certain species of primitive ape do, using the hands to grasp, for example, tree branches as successive launching pads. 'How many times do I have to tell you? No brachiation at Sunday School until after the last hymn, Roderick!'

BRACHYDROMIC *a.* Following a deflected path in relation to the target. Said of missiles that miss or fall short. 'Brandon, must you be ever brachydromic? The way to the car is straight across the road, not via the ice-creamery down the street.'

BRIGANDINE *n.* A medieval coat of mail, made of metal rings, studs and strips sewn onto a leather jacket. In today's world, the perfect term for a bikie's jacket. Not to be confused with *brigantine*, a two-masted vessel which is square-rigged on the foremast and fore-and-aft rigged on the mainmast, and which is hardly ever worn by bikies.

BRUXISM *n.* Abnormal grinding of teeth. 'OK, it's agreed, then! Ten dollars from each of us to whoever manages to provoke Daddy to bruxism stage?'

BULLARIUM *n.* A collection of Papal Bulls, i.e., authoritative edicts sealed with a *bulla*, or lead seal, by the Pope. 'Children, this is our first family conference for the year, and in your father's absence I'd like to suggest that it would be a nice surprise for him if we put together a bullarium of his collected statements on domestic management, child behaviour and the weather, and affixed them to the door of his beer fridge in the garage.'

BUTYRACEOUS *a.* Looking or acting like butter; buttery. 'Who was that oily young man who took Sabrina out last week? The one who complimented you on your hairdo?' 'Oh, the butyraceous one! That was …'

C

CABALA *n.* Hebrew mystical theology. Hence, any secret, arcane or occult system. Your husband's filing cabinet.

CACOSMIA *n.* A condition in which the sufferer experiences awful tastes and smells without any external physical cause. (In the later stages of his brain tumour, George Gershwin constantly experienced the smell of burning rubber.) 'Yes, I know it's an awful smell, dear, but don't worry, it's not cacosmia, it's just that you-know-who has just passed this way.'

CADUCOUS *a.* (In botany and zoology) dropping away, falling off or perishing at an early stage of development. 'So this is the latest in your succession of caducous boyfriends, Miranda?'

CANONICAL AGE *phr.* The minimum age, as laid down in canonical law (i.e., church law), for ordination or for the performance of a specified function in the church. 'So Damon wants the car keys again, eh?

Tell him my answer's the same – when he reaches canonical age, and not before!'

CARPENTUM *n.* A two-wheeled carriage of ancient times, often covered with an awning. Perhaps a useful term now for one of those electrically driven wheelchairs for the crippled elderly. Or, even better, for your hobby-farmer neighbour's dinky little tractor: 'Ah, taking the carpetum out for a run, Frank? Oh – wait a moment – I didn't notice those two little wheels at the back! What are they – some kind of, like, trainer wheels?'

CAVITATION *n.* The forming of cavities within an otherwise continuous material, as for example behind a solid object that is moving through a fluid, or within a solid object as a result of bombardment with sound waves. 'Don't expect too much of Jamie, mother. All those rock concerts ... first his hearing, now the cavitation in his brain ... I warned him this would happen ...'

CERATE *n.* A medicated waxy *unguent* (q.v.). 'Warning! Warning! Your father is preparing to dice the vegetables with the new super-sharp knife! Bring the cerates and the unguents!'

CEROSCOPY *n.* Divination by means of melted wax. The wax is poured into cold water, and the diviner predicts the future on the basis of the shapes taken by the congealed wax. If you are nervous about the outcome of the experiment, you could of course perform ceroscopy to find out what the result of the ceroscopy would be. Are you with me here?

CHASMUS HYSTERICUS *phr.* Hysterical yawning. 'I'm not bored, really I'm not – it's my chasmus; gets me every time when I get too excited.'

CHEIROPOMPHOLYX *n.* A disease in which blisters filled with fluid suddenly appear on the patient's skin. 'Of course I hold no grudges, Helen; in fact I wish you the greatest cheiropompholyx for as long as you live.'

CIRRIPED *n.* A member of an order of crustaceans which in their adult stage attach themselves in a parasitic way to other creatures or objects. As, for example, barnacles. 'Dearest, do you think Kimberley might leave home this year and get her own little flat – or is she to be our permanent cirriped?'

CLAIRAUDIENCE *n.* The aural equivalent of clairvoyance. In other words, the hearing of sounds that are too far removed in time or space to be perceived by the physical mechanisms of hearing. 'So this is the club auditorium? Oh my God, I feel … there are terrible emanations from the past, all about us here … I hear line-dancing music! I hear Scottish country dance music! I hear … dear God, this is too much to bear … I hear junior elocution competitions! I hear the sound of a Little Miss Beauty prizegiving! For God's sake, get me out of here! Curse this damned clairaudience of mine!'

CLEDONISM *n.* The use of euphemistic language to avoid the untoward magical effects that might be caused by the use of plain language. Referring to the Devil, for example, as 'Monsieur', in the belief that the simple fellow will not realise he is being spoken about and therefore will have no occasion to join the group. A reference to a spouse as 'His Lordship' or 'Her Ladyship' could be regarded as cledonism.

clishnaclaver

CLISHNACLAVER *n.* Silly gossip. Another of those Scottish words. Why are they all so pejorative?

CLYSTER *n.* An enema, or other form of intestinal injection. 'No, I cannot offer you a donation at this time,' you inform the telemarketer who has phoned you at your home during dinner on behalf of an imperfectly identified charity; 'but if you were to send your representative around I would be glad to give him a substantial clyster.'

COMPURGATION *n.* The exoneration of an accused party purely on the basis of oaths sworn by a number of other persons (presumably his friends). An ancient practice that could well be revived in the next World Cup soccer competition. 'We claim compurgation!' could be the cry of the team when one of their number is about to be dismissed from the field for illegal play.

CONCINNITY *n.* Elegance and appropriateness of style. See, for example, any volume published by David R. Godine, Publisher, Incorporated.

COPIOPIA *n.* Hysterical eye-strain. Condition of a lexicographer. But a lovely word to say aloud. Try it.

COPULATIVE CONJUNCTION *phr.* Not, not what you think at all. In grammar, this is the correct name for the co-ordinative conjunction. Still in the dark? Our old friend, the word 'and'. 'And what's more, you children, not only the way you behave but especially the way you talk needs a lot of improvement. For a start, I expect more copulative conjunctions from both of you!'

CORVÉE *n.* A feudal duty to serve one's master; hence, any system of forced labour. 'Kitchen duty for you tonight, Kristen! No, it's no use pouting and sulking. You know the terms of your corvée!'

CRYPTOCLIMATE *n.* The climate found within a small enclosed structure, as distinct from the local climate generally (microclimate) and the wider regional climate (macroclimate). 'You seriously expect me to go into Shane's room? Have you any idea what the cryptoclimate in there is like?'

CRYPTOMNESIA *n.* The spontaneous revival of former memories, experiences, facts and items of knowledge, without any ability to recall the circumstances which originally attended them. 'I'm sure I know her, but who is she? And how big a fool did I make of myself in her presence? Introduce me if you must, but I may have to plead cryptomnesia.'

CURSORIAL *a.* Suited to walking or running as a method of locomotion, as distinct from other methods such as swimming, flying, slithering, etc. 'What can be said in favour of Luke? Let us think for a moment. Well, for a start, he is cursorial, definitely cursorial. And then there's ... now, let me think ... just give me a moment here ...'

cursorial

CYMLIN *n.* A kind of squash, i.e., an edible gourd, giving rise to the obvious possibilities for its use in relation to that other squash, the tennis-like game played indoors with a small, painful rubber ball. 'Cyril and I are just going off by ourselves for a few hours to cymlinate.'

CYNOPHOBIA *n.* The morbid dread of dogs. Condition of cats and postmen.

CYPRINOID *a.* Carp-like. 'Entertaining another of your cyprinoid friends with your DVD equipment, Desmond? Wouldn't he be more interested in spending some time with our goldfish?'

cynophobia

D

DECAPSULATION *n.* The removal of the enveloping membrane of an organ. No, not the unpacking of a Korean musical instrument from its polythene wrapping, but one of those unspeakable things that surgeons and pathologists do. 'And another thing, young lady! Before you set foot outside that door, I'd like to see a little decapsulation brought to bear on that thickly made-up face of yours!'

DECARCERATION *n.* The freeing of criminals and the mentally ill from confinement in gaols and asylums, and their reinstatement in society at large, thereby making it harder for the rest of us to tell who are the politicians.

DECONSTRUCTION *n.* An approach to the analysis of text, popular in the 1970s and associated in particular with one Jacques Derrida, who asserted that the text means something very different from what it appears to mean, whether to the reader *or the author* (my italics). No-one said out loud that this emperor had no clothes, but if the technique of deconstruction were applied to Derrida's own writings about deconstruction then it would presumably become apparent that deconstruction must be something completely different from what it is said to be.

DEFEASIBILITY *n.* In philosophy, said of a belief or statement which is open to being refuted by evidence that may be forthcoming in the future. As for example, 'I am going to enjoy myself today.' In contradistinction to *incorrigibility*, which is said of a belief or statement which events cannot possibly show to have been wrong. As for example, 'Peter Bowler is the supreme lexicographer of our time.' (An earlier example of incorrigibility was thought to be Descartes' 'I exist'; but the passage of time has proved him to be wrong.)

DEIPNOSOPHIST *n.* A wise conversationalist at the dinner table. Unfortunately, the two elements of the definition rarely go together. The author, for example, claims to meet one of the two criteria (he refuses to say which) but not the other.

DEMOPHOBIA *n.* The morbid dread of crowds. Most of us are demophobes at some time, or in some circumstances. Pity those who are also *autophobes* (q.v.).

DENDROCHRONOLOGY *n.* The process of dating a tree by counting its annual growth rings as shown in a cross-section. 'How old, you ask, do I think Isabella is? No problem – dendrochronology will give us the answer! Just give me a cross-section of her, will you, and I'll get to work.'

DESULTOR *n.* In ancient Rome, the desultor was a circus performer who rode two horses at the same time, alternately leaping from one to the other. Today an estate agent, perhaps? A politician?

DEUTERAGONIST *n.* In ancient Greek drama, the second most important actor, i.e., the actor next in importance to the protagonist. 'Let me make one thing perfectly clear – in this kitchen, I am the protagonist and you are the deuteragonist.'

DHARNA *n.* In eastern civilisations, a method of claiming justice by fasting, to death if need be, before the door of the oppressor from or against whom justice is being sought. In western civilisations we have, of course, the Teenager's Sulk. 'James, the concept of dharna, which you have so ably introduced into this little disagreement with your parents, certainly covers the refusal to eat your vegetables, but it does not extend to your taking regular trips down the road to the nearest fast-food outlet.'

DIALYSIS *n.* A word with two quite different meanings. You all know about the medical one. The other is a method of analytical argument in which all the possible pros and cons are brought forward and one by one despatched by sheer logic. 'So, Shelly – the proposal is that you go out tonight to the wet T-shirt competition down at the football club. Well, let's apply the dialysis process to this one and see where we end up.'

DICK TEST *phr.* Not what you might think at all, but rather a test of one's susceptibility to, or immunity from, scarlet fever. The test, believe it or not, consists of the injection under the skin of streptococcus toxins, and is named after George and Gladys Dick, who presumably came up with the idea. I think we'll leave that one right there.

DISBRANCH *v.* Superior Person's word for 'prune' (i.e., trim a tree or bush).

DISFELLOWSHIPPING *n.* Excommunication from those who hold certain belief systems, such as Seventh Day Adventists, Urantians, etc. 'Go to your room, young man! It's disfellowshipping for you until you've taken down those Black Sabbath posters and cleaned under the bed!'

DISSILIENT *a.* Bursting or springing open. 'I'm returning these shorts for a refund. The zip is irredeemably dissilient.'

DIVULSION *n.* The act of pulling or wrenching apart. 'OK, that's the end of that video. Switch on the

divulsion

lights, and let's see how much divulsion we need to bring to bear on Jason and Rachel.'

DOXY *n.* A prostitute; also, surprisingly, a belief or religious doctrine. See how you can use these terms for maximum confusion.

DROMOMANIA *n.* A pathological urge to travel. In its most serious state, leads to membership of the International Olympics Committee.

DROMOPHOBIA *n.* The morbid dread of travel, particularly when experienced in the form of a pathological fear of crossing streets. In the case of certain streets in Paris, Bangkok or Rome, an understandable condition.

DRUMBLE *v.* To move slowly, reluctantly and sluggishly. Mode of locomotion of the teenager called to the dinner table.

DUUMVIRATE *n.* The exercise of governmental power by two people acting together. 'This isn't a family! This is a duumvirate! What happened to democracy?' (Suggested parting lines for teenager storming out of the room.)

DYMAXION *n.* Name given by Buckminster Fuller, the famous American engineer, to his concept of the maximum net performance per gross energy input. 'You're asking me to relate Owen's work performance to his gross energy input, as part of his annual staff appraisal? It's his dymaxion? Listen, Buckminster Fuller may know all about buildings, but . . . "gross energy input"? . . . the term has no meaning in Owen's case.'

DYSPHORIA *n.* Depression, pathological discontent. Opposite of *euphoria*, or extreme happiness. The novelist Thomas Hardy once told a friend that he would not read *Wuthering Heights*, because he 'had been told that it was depressing'.

DYSTELEOLOGY *n.* The metaphysical doctrine that events have no pre-ordained purpose; that there is no 'final cause'. 'Let's see, who'll be my navigator for this trip? I think in view of Mummy's lifelong adherence to dysteleology, we'd better not give her the map this time, eh, Kylie?'

E

ECLIPSIS *n.* Omitting a grammatically necessary word or form. A whole generation of young people has, for instance, been taught in college courses laughably called 'Communication' to do without the conjunction 'that', and so we have sentences such as 'He said the end was near.' Next, the 'the' and the 'was' will go, and our language will have finally reached the 'me Tarzan, you Jane' level.

ECPHONEMA *n.* An exclamation engendered by a sudden emotion, such as joy, wonder or horror. 'OK Mum, so I've passed in mathematics. This time can we do without the ecphonema?'

EDAPHOLOGY *n.* The science of soil as a plant-growing medium. 'You don't want a carpet-cleaning firm for Rodney's room, Mum, you need an edaphologist.'

EFFLATION *n.* An emanation that is breathed or blown out. 'Ah, my darling, I can tell that you are repelled by my alliaceous efflations! If only you too had chosen the garlic mussels as a main!'

EMPORIATRICS *n.* The science of travellers' health. Embraces such aspects as jet lag, exotic infections, over-exposure to heat or cold, altitude sickness, etc. Next time when you're asking for travel insurance, ask them to include full emporiatric cover; you may get away with it, even with your heart condition.

ENANTIOPATHY *n.* A disease or affliction which protects you from another. Similarly, the curing of the latter disease by inducing the former. 'We simply must divert Anthony from his fixation with that appalling Mrs Sandalbath; why don't we try locking him – sort of accidentally, if you know what I mean – in the broom cupboard with that nice little Miriam girl from next door? She should be adequately enantiopathic, don't you think?'

ENJAMBEMENT *n.* A literary term, denoting the running on of meaning from the end of one line of a poem to the beginning of the next. 'I don't know, Raelene; I just find Metallica lyrics so ... so *ordinary* after the Stones. Where's all the enjambement?'

Epicedium

EPICEDIUM *n.* A song of mourning sung over a corpse. 'And so, once again, let me express our hopes and expectations to our elected representative for the coming sittings. It is our fondest desire, sir, that by the end of your term we will be enjoying our epicedium here in our little town.'

EPIPLEXIS *n.* A kind of argument that begins by insulting the other person, or by trying to bully or shame him into agreeing with you. 'If only you had the brains of a marsupial, you would surely see that .... ' May bring on a reaction involving extreme emotion; this is called apoplexy.

EPISTAXIS *n.* Superior Person's word for a nosebleed.

EQUIPOLLENT *a.* Equivalent (in size, strength, weight, effect, etc.). 'So what if your father said you could go out with that Mitch boy? You don't for a moment imagine that your father and I are equipollent in terms of household decisions, do you?'

ERUMPENT *a.* Breaking or bursting out through the skin, as do certain fungus spores. 'And when my friends come round here tonight for our pyjama party, for God's sake stay in your room, Jefferson! I don't know whether you realise it, but you're more than usually erumpent today!'

ESTOVERS *n.* Those necessities of life that may legally be taken by a tenant for his own use, as, for example, firewood from his landlord's property. 'Mum, can we officially declare the fudge brownies in the fridge to be estovers?'

EUDEMONIA *n.* A state of absolute happiness, well-being and good fortune. A purely theoretical concept.

EVERRICULUM *n.* A fishing net. (From the Latin 'to sweep out'.) 'Got everything, dear? Suntan cream, bucket, spade, towel, goggles, flippers, your little everriculum?'

EVITABLE *a.* That which may be avoided. 'Who, me? Accompany you to the mall for white-goods comparison shopping, darling? I think that's absolutely evitable, don't you?'

EXCITABLE DELMA *n.* At the outset, I must make it clear that this is not one of the author's childish fabrications. Excitable Delma is the name of a lizard (scientific name *delma tincta*) found in open woodland or grassland. Called excitable because of its vigorous writhing when disturbed, the Excitable Delma is a member of the Pygopodidae family, i.e., a legless lizard. Treasure this knowledge, because one day, with any luck at all, you will meet a human Delma who happens to fit the specifications.

EXODONTIA *n.* That part of dentistry which relates to the extraction or knocking out of teeth. 'You may think, sir, that you have a prior claim on this parking space merely because you have so aggressively driven your car at high speed across the bows of my own, but I assure you that you will retain this space at the expense of immediate exodontia.'

EXOGAMY *n.* Marriage outside of a certain group, as laid down by law or custom. As for example the prohibitions in various societies on marriage to one's close relatives, to someone of the same sex, etc. 'I think in Willoughby's case the principle of exogamy would not rule out marriage to an orangutan, don't you?'

exodontia

F

FABRILIA *n.* A collective term for all the various types of tools used by a craftsman. 'If you leave your fabrilia all over the basement floor, don't expect me to clean it!'

FALLIBILISM *n.* The philosophical doctrine that it is not necessary for our beliefs to be established as absolutely certain beyond all possibility of doubt. 'No, I think we will take the road to the left, darling, despite all your protestations to the contrary. My fallibilism gives me strength.'

FANTASMAGORIA *n.* A changing, incoherent series of apparitions or fantasms. Late-night television. The Superior Person always spells the word with a *ph*, not an *f*, thus: phantasmagoria.

FASCIATION *n.* Bandaging; or becoming bound up. 'I find that you have an overpowering fascination for me, Mrs Boddington. Every second Tuesday, perhaps – say, about 3 p.m.?'

FIMBRIATED *a.* Having a fringe. 'Why are Brooke's boyfriends always so damned . . . fimbriated?'

FLOCCILLATION *n.* The action of a feverish patient in picking at the bedclothes during his or her delirium. 'I know your father has been under a lot of stress lately, Bettina, but in future will you *please* try to remember – we don't call in the men in white coats until actual floccillation sets in!'

FORTUITISM *n.* The metaphysical doctrine that chance rules – that things happen according to fortune rather than in pursuance of rational design or principle. 'Well, dear, considering the way the twins turned out, I think we must draw all the strength we can from our fortuitism, don't you?'

FOUR-FLUSH *n.* A poker hand consisting of four cards of the same suit, the fifth being of another suit. This hand has no value at all in poker. When your opponent lays his cards down, showing a pair, if you quickly show yours, calling out, 'Four flush,' and sweeping the money off the table immediately, saying simultaneously, 'Who's next deal?' you just might get away with it. If you do, you will have become a four-flusher, or sneaky bluff-artist.

FRONDIFEROUS *a.* Frond-bearing. Condition of the face of the pubescent male.

FROWARD *a.* Uncooperative, contrary. One who fails to agree with the present author.

FUGACITY *n.* Fleetingness, volatility; the tendency towards transience – to changing or moving on quickly. 'It's nice that Maybelle has so many boyfriends, dear, but their universal fugacity is a little worrying, don't you think? Can it be something to do with her dasypygality? I mean, having all that hair down there is not her fault; it's just one of the realities of genetics, isn't it?'

FUMAROLE *n.* A small hole from which volcanic vapours issue. The potential for metaphoric use of the term is too evident to be dwelt upon here.

FUMATORIUM *n.* An airtight chamber used for fumigation. 'If you want your brother, Annabel, I believe you will find him in the fumatorium, or, as he laughably calls it, his bedroom, in a state of substance-induced euphoria.'

FURCULUM *n.* Wishbone. 'Come on, let's you and I do the furculum together.' Knowing your penchant for deceptive language, your dinner-table companion is, for the nonce, nonplussed.

FURUNCLE *n.* A boil or similarly inflamed sore caused by bacterial infection. 'All right, then, Harrington; if your principles prevent you from donating to our charity for retired authors, that's perfectly understandable. Off you go, then – and all the very best of furuncles to you, old chap!'

G

GALERICULATE *a.* Covered by a hat. 'Here comes Lawrence . . . and, good heavens, he's galericulate! The alopecia must really be getting to him!'

GELASMUS *n.* Hysterical laughter. 'Hope the sermon goes well today, dear; and don't worry so much about it – I'm sure you'll get lots of gelasmus from the congregation!'

GENOPHOBIA *n.* The morbid dread of sex. Condition of the average male teenager's girlfriend. Or so he likes to think.

GILLIVER *n.* A wanton wench. 'What is this "gilliver" you have on your Christmas gift wish list, Morris?'

GIMBAL *n.* A device used on board ship at sea, usually consisting of two movable rings as seating for a compass or other device to keep it as stable as possible. Also a form of rod holder used in game fishing, consisting of a movable socket in a protuberance fixed to a belt and hanging just below the waist. 'Daddy, what does Mummy mean when she says that your gimbal would be good for holding a dildo in?'

GLOSSECTOMY *n.* The removal, partial or complete, of the tongue. 'You're being a little unfair to Mrs Wambuddy, aren't you? I mean – sure, she does go on a bit – but there's nothing wrong with the way she talks that a little glossectomy wouldn't fix.'

Gorgonise

GNOMIC *a.* Pithy and epigrammatic (said of remarks), sometimes leaning towards the self-consciously witty, sometimes towards the sententious. Thus a *gnomology* is a collection of gnomic sayings. 'So, children, I see that when the cat's away ...' 'Wait a minute, Dad – Stacey, get out the gnomology, quick! And get a pen! Now – go on, Dad ...'

GOMPHOSIS *n.* Technical term for the connection of two bodily elements by the firm implantation of one in a socket situated in the other. As, for example, a tooth in a jaw. The potential metaphorical uses of the term are too evident, and indeed too indelicate, for the author to specify in a work of this nature.

GONAPOPHYSES *n.* A collective term for the genital organs of insects generally. 'Welcome to our sorority dance, Dean Archworthy. The refreshments are at the end table; and over there, standing along the wall near the fire exit, those boys are our guests from the fraternities – the gonapophyses, as we call them.'

GORGONISE *v.* To petrify or paralyse, as if by the gaze of the Gorgon Medusa. 'Mormons at the door, Charlotte – up you get and gorgonise them, quick, before they get started!'

GOZINTA BOXES *phr.* An item of magical equipment consisting of two boxes, which, though clearly the same size, will alternately fit inside each other – an apparent impossibility. The derivation? Each box gozinta the other. I am not making this up. Ask any magician.

GRAVISPHERE *n.* The spherical space within which a body's gravitational field is overpowering. 'Watch out! You're getting close to her gravisphere!' you cry, as your friend backs, all unawares, towards a fully bedizened matron at the annual DAR Ball.

GUBERNACULUM *n.* A rudder; originally a broad-bladed oar, one of which was placed at each side of the boat. 'Hard left on the gubernaculum! The gubernaculum, Daddy, the gubernaculum, for God's sake!' is the cry as your father approaches the door jamb when backing out of the garage in his new Mercedes Benz for the first time.

GUGUSSE *n.* According to Mrs Byrne's amazing dictionary, a gugusse is 'a young, effeminate man who trysts with priests'. Can such things be? And can you say 'trysts with priests' three times quickly?

GUTTATE *a.* Covered in coloured spots like little drops of liquid. Another unkind one for pimply people.

GYNECOCRACY *n.* Goverment by a woman or by women; the supremacy of the female. Well, if there's a word for it, it must exist, mustn't it? The ontological argument for the supremacy of women. I'm a believer.

H

HABILIMENTS *n.* Superior Person's word for items of clothing.

HAEMOPHOBIA *n.* The morbid dread of blood. Most commonly encountered, in the age of the human immunodeficiency virus, in the world of surgeons and nurses – ironically, those whose occupation renders it the most disabling.

HAGIOSCOPE *n.* An oblique opening beside the chancel-arch of a church, to provide a view of the high altar. Sometimes called a 'squint'. 'Ah, at the old hagio-scope again, eh, Lachlan?' you might say, on catching your young brother peering around the edge of his bedroom curtain at the young lady who has come to live opposite. 'Be careful – too much of that and you'll have a squint.'

HAPHALGESIA *n.* A condition in which the patient suffers torments from the mere pressure of clothing or weight of bedclothes. 'So, Craig – you are seriously intending to go out to line dancing tonight wearing your cowboy boots, your leather jacket, your trench coat, and on top of that your Russian winter headgear. Why in God's name would you want to suffer all the symptoms of haphalgesia without actually having it?'

HAPTEPHOBIA *n.* The morbid dread of being touched. Condition of . . . (see *genophobia*).

HARMATIA *n.* (From the Greek word for 'error'.) A literary term referring to the fatal error, either from moral shortcoming or from ignorance, which ultimately destroys a great man, or woman, in tragic literature. Othello's jealousy, Hamlet's indecision, etc. In the words of the chorus in *Dido and Aeneas*, 'great minds against themselves conspire'. Why not propose, for your next assignment in Media Studies 111A, 'The Role of Harmatia in the Character of Tim-the-Tool-Man Taylor'?

HEALFANG *n.* The pillory. 'Mummy, Amanda and I have made a lovely little healfang in the back yard. Would it be all right if we put the baby in it for a while?'

haptephobia

HEDONICS *n.* The science of active enjoyment and pleasure. There's a science of this? Where can I enrol?

HELMINTHOLOGY *n.* The study of parasitic worms. Some universities give courses in this and call it Political Science.

HERMENEUTICS *n.* The art of interpreting the Scriptures or other ambiguous texts. 'OK, we've got the new mobile phone out of its box, and here's the little fifty-page booklet with the miniaturised ideographic instructions. Charles, you're the one who's done hermeneutics at college. Get to work on it, and we'll see you in the morning.'

HETAERISM *n.* Promiscuous living and sleeping with women to whom one is not married. Ah, sweet dream of youth.

HIBERNACULUM *n.* A case in which to hiberate (i.e., sleep through an inactive period such as winter), put together by certain insects from found materials. 'Pyjama party tomorrow night! Everyone got sleeping bags you can bring? Oh, all right, Candice, your hibernaculum, then.'

HILARODY *n.* Not a misspelling of *hilarity*, but something not far removed from that. Hilarody is a form of ancient Greek mime in which some great tragedy is made fun of. A burlesque. 'Oh, most amusing! I come home covered in mud after having to deal with two flat tyres in the rain, getting towed away, using all my remaining money for new tyres

43

and waiting for two hours to get the job done. And all you can greet me with is hilarody.'

HISPID *a.* Rough with stiff hairs or bristles. 'Have you shaved, or are you still hispid? And if the latter, don't tell me that "it's a statement". That won't wash with me.'

HISTRION *n.* An actor. The adjective *histrionic* today carries implications of exaggeration in acting style, and in the eighteenth century a histrion was someone who played the buffoon. Perhaps well illustrated in the person of Robert Coates, universally known in his time as 'Romeo Coates' because he specialised in the role of Romeo, which he played in a blue silk coat covered with spangles, a Charles II wig and a top hat. In playing the death scene, he would first carefully sweep with his silk handkerchief the spot on stage where he intended to fall; then remove his hat and set it neatly beside him on the floor; then take several minutes in lying down, turning around and about until he had found the most comfortable position. Audiences hysterical with laughter would demand, and receive, numerous encores of this scene. According to Caufield, contemporary reports of his acting style describe him as having 'an inflexibility of limb, an awkwardness of gait, and an idiotic manner of standing still which evoked hysteria even before he opened his mouth to speak.'

HOCKTIDE *n.* Otherwise known as Hoke Day, an annual festival held in the English town Hungerford in the week following the second Tuesday after Easter. According to T. Sharper Knowlson's *The Origins of*

Popular Superstitions and Customs (1930), on the Tuesday of the festival the women bind the men. According to my other source, the *AA Illustrated Guide to Britain*, a somewhat more recent publication, a team of 'tutti men' go around town with a posy of flowers on a stick, collecting kisses from the women. Either way, it sounds like a lot of fun. 'So, Miss Purdue, here we are alone together. Did you know that today is Hocktide? We should celebrate it in the traditional fashion, don't you think? Which will it be – the rope or the pole?'

HOROLOGY *n.* The study of time. Not as easy as you think: have you ever thought really hard about the International Date Line? The actor Patrick MacNee, of *Avengers* fame, told the story of the time his death was mistakely announced on US television. 'When they rang my daughter, she said that couldn't be right, because she had just been talking to me on the phone a few minutes ago in Australia. They said: "No, he's dead. It's just the time difference."'

HORRIPILATION *n.* A feeling of cold, accompanied by goose pimples and bristling hair. 'Thank you for asking me out, Brent, but I just can't. Please don't be hurt. The thought of going out with you gives me genuine horripilation, it really does; but I've got a prior engagement, I'm afraid.'

HURLEY-HACKET *n.* Archaic and therefore Superior Person's word for a sledge or toboggan.

HYDROPHOBIA *n.* The morbid dread of water. Experienced by rabies victims because of the agony of swallowing. Also experienced by the teenage male, who, offered water to drink, will reject it in favour of any other available liquid.

HYLOTHEISM *n.* The belief that God is the whole of the material universe in which we live. An uncomfortable faith to hold, given the purposes to which we put certain objects. And, of course, the existence of cockroaches.

HYPERPROSEXIA *n.* The concentrating and focusing of what would otherwise be normal human powers of observation to such a high degree that extraordinary achievements in perception are possible. As seen for instance in the ability of Australian Aboriginal trackers to follow trails which are imperceptible to others. 'I sometimes wish, Damien, that you would direct your powers of hyperprosexia to your schoolwork rather than to the comparative study of zombie-film make-up artists.'

HYPERTHYMIC *a.* In a state of morbidly exaggerated activity of mind or body. 'Hmm, I see hyperthymia has not set in yet,' you remark as you pass by your deeply encouched teenager on your way through the TV room.

HYPETHRAL *a.* Without a roof, open to the sky; as for example a building uncompleted or partly demolished. A suitably inoffensive descriptor for your balder friends.

HYPNOPAEDIA *n.* Training or instruction during sleep. 'Good morning, class! Are we to start today with the usual half-hour of hypnopaedia?'

HYPNOPHOBIA *n.* The morbid dread of falling asleep. Especially when you're sitting right across the table from the guest speaker.

HYPOCORISM *n.* The use of nicknames and similar familiarities, as in 'honey, I'm home!' or 'good old Charlie Dickens would have written it differently'. From the Greek for 'playing the child'. 'And another thing – do you really have to ask me every evening if I'd like a "drinkie-poo"? I mean, I expect a certain amount of hypocorism from you, but this is pathetic!'

HYPOPLASIA *n.* Arrested development. Condition of a collector of empty beer cans, a golfer, a line dancer, etc.

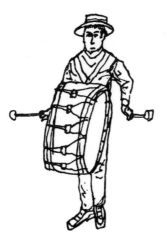

hypnopaedia

I

IDIOLECT *n.* A collective term for all the distinctive speech habits that are characteristic of a particular individual. 'Do you think it's really wise for Rodney to drop English? I mean, his idiolect has barely passed the *phatic* (q.v.) stage, has it not?'

IGNIFY *v.* To burn or set something alight. 'Yes, I have indeed studied the new draft mission statement and corporate code of ethics, Mr Malperson; in fact I've had it put up on the section notice board, and I'll see that it's thoroughly ignified.'

ILLOCUTIONARY *a.* In linguistics, an act carried out as an intrinsic consequence of an utterance, as for example the performance of a baptism ceremony, or the fulfilment of a promise. 'You remember what I said I would do to you, young man, if you disobeyed your parents and failed to attend Sunday school this morning? And you remember my mention of the word "illocutionary"? You will not, then, be surprised to hear me say now that I hereby baptise you with this garden hose.'

49

IMBRICATED *a.* The manner in which roof shingles, or, say, fish scales, are laid down in an overlapping manner so that the breaks between them are at least partly covered, protecting the structure beneath. 'Is she fully imbricated and ready to go?' you ask the hairdresser when you drop in to pick up your best beloved.

IMPEDITIVE *a.* Getting in the way, causing obstruction. A little something for that difference of opinion at the traffic lights. 'You impeditive moron!'

IMPOSTHUME *n.* An abscess. Nice eighteenth-century word for a nasty pre-penicillin affliction. 'It's been wonderful having you with us, Martin; "go quickly, come back slowly", as they say in the Gaelic – a lovely saying, isn't it? – and may you have all the imposthumes in the world!'

IMPUDICITY *n.* Shamelessness, lack of modesty. 'You ask me about Briony's potential as a TV talk-show presenter? Hmm, let me think. Well, she certainly has all the necessary impudicity …'

IMPUTRESCIBLE *a.* Not subject to corruption. 'It is my pleasant duty to introduce to you all tonight our local candidate for the coming election. Not all of you know him as well as I do, so let me say right away that imputrescibility is totally foreign to his nature …'

INDEX EXPURGATORIUS *phr.* We all know about the *Index Librorum Prohibitorum*, i.e., the list of books forbidden to Catholics, but you may not have heard of this one. It is the official Catholic list of specific passages which must be deleted from a book before it can be read by the faithful. What a wonderful idea, to have a guide to all the best naughty bits! But where can I get a copy?

INFRA DIGNITATEM *phr.* Always use this, the full version. Never just say 'infra dig'.

INQUILINE *a.* Dwelling in another's place of abode, as for example an insect occupying a gall already chosen as home by another. 'I don't mind your mother coming to town occasionally to visit us, but I have to say I wish she wasn't so damned inquiline.'

INTERPELLATION *n.* A formal demand made upon a member of a government to explain an official act or policy. How many of you knew you could do that? Get cracking! Lodge those interpellations right now!

INTINCTION *n.* Delivering both elements of the Eucharist at once, by dipping the bread into the wine. The Superior Person's word for cookie-dunking.

INTROJECTION *n.* A term from the Magic Land of Psychoanalysis, defined thus: 'the incorporation into the ego of mental images of persons or objects to the extent of being emotionally affected by them'. (Or, in plain English, liking someone or something.)

IOTA *n.* A tiny particle. From *iota*, the Greek letter corresponding to the English *i*. Received perhaps its most charming use from John Barrett, Professor of

Oriental Languages at Trinity College, Dublin, in the late eighteenth century. One of his finest achievements was the discovery, hidden away in the folds of another manuscript, of an ancient Greek text of the Gospel of St Matthew. Barrett had been glancing at a pile of papers when he noticed (in his own words) 'a dear little iota in the corner'. Barrett spoke and wrote ancient Greek and Latin with absolute fluency, but his English was appalling. He lived within the walls of the College from the age of fourteen, and had virtually no knowledge of the outside world, and, from all accounts, no common sense at all. He once had two holes, one big and one small, cut in his door to allow access for his two cats, one of which was big and one small, because it had not occurred to him that the small cat would be able to go through the big hole.

ISONOMY *n.* Equality of civil rights, status in the community, etc. 'I hate to shatter your illusions, Debbie, but this household is not a democracy, nor do you have isonomy with your parents. You will not, I repeat not, be going to the football team's end-of-season party.'

ISOPYCNIC *a.* Equally dense (said of different mediums such as a liquid or gas). 'Who wants Hayley and Harvey on their team? They're isopycnic, you know.'

J

JACK-A-DANDY *n.* A ridiculously foppish person. A television chef, an art critic, a society butterfly, etc.

jaculate

JACULATE *v.* To throw, especially a spear or dart. Throwing the used plastic picnic cutlery into the waste bin at the park, you call back to the car: 'OK, Miranda, I've jaculated, and I'm ready to go.'

JAGUARUNDI *n.* A flesh-eating weasel-like wildcat of the tropical Americas. If you know any weasel-like wildcats, this is the word for them.

JANIZARY *n.* (Sometimes spelt janissary.) In former times, a member of the Turkish Sultan's corps of bodyguards. Originally, these were young law-breakers who had been taken out of prison and trained for their duties. Perhaps a good term for the well-dressed young men with grim faces who crowd around United States Presidents at all times (except in windowless rooms at the White House).

JEHU *n.* Everyone knows this term in the sense of a coach driver; but the primary sense is of a furiously *fast* driver. (Pronounced 'geehew', by the way, with the emphasis on the 'gee'.) 'So, will Daddy drive or will we place our lives in Timothy's hands? What a choice – between the tardigrade and the jehu!'

JIGGER *n.* One of those brilliant words with a multitude of meanings and therefore ideal for confusing, or at least vaguely unsettling, the person being spoken to. A jigger can be: one who jigs, i.e., dances; a machine for separating ores; a potter's wheel; a small sail; a small mast; a golf club; a billiards bridge; a measuring glass for liquor; a flea or mite that burrows into the skin; or any small device the proper name for which is not known. I love words like this. 'So Megan's into Irish dancing now? Ah, I bet she's a right little jigger!'

JOCOSE *a.* Having the quality of a joke. Notice that this is not quite the same as *jocular* (joking/in joking mood) or *jocund* (in merry mood). One of Dr Johnson's eating and drinking companions, the actor David Garrick, grew disenchanted with the good

Doctor's habit of imposing heavy witticisms on the gathering, and henceforth, whenever Johnson silenced those around him with one of his pontifical witticisms, Garrick would unsmilingly remark, quietly but audibly, 'Oh, most jocose, most jocose!'

JUGUM *n.* A yoke for cattle. Also a metaphorical expression for the yoke imposed by Roman rule over its conquered peoples. When your father enters the kitchen after his day's work and happens to ask your mother what she thinks he should wear for the evening, you pipe up: 'A jugum, I should imagine.'

JUKES, THE *n.* The pseudonym adopted by researchers for a real-life New York family who were the subject of a major psychological and sociological study in the nineteenth century. The study took the Jukes, who had an abnormally high incidence among their family members of criminal behaviour, poverty and disease, and followed them over several generations, showing that this pattern persisted through every generation studied. On meeting your new in-laws for the first time: 'Are you related to the Jukes at all, by any chance? No? Oh, it's just that I thought I saw a resemblance there for a moment.'

JUSSIVE *a.* A grammatical concept, originating in the Semitic languages, signifying that a verb is being used in a mood (in the grammatical sense) of mild command. But listen, guys: I've used the jussive mood many times, talking to my work colleagues, to my wife, to my children, to visiting tradesmen . . . and let me tell you, it doesn't work.

K

KAMALA *n.* The reddish powder obtained from the fruit of an Indian tree so named. Used as a strong purgative. 'A little kamala on your couscous?' you solicitously enquire of your pretentious *soi-disant* gourmet acquaintance over dinner at the latest preciously exotic restaurant.

KANOON *n.* An early instrument, being a type of dulcimer having fifty or so strings and played with the fingers. A little like a giant-size zither. Your little niece Cecily comes to visit, accompanied by her mother, who as usual insists on the child's showing off her latest party piece on the piano, the seemingly interminable Durand Waltz in E-flat major. 'Ah,' you say, vigorously ruffling the child's hair with your hand – a thing you know she hates – 'in my day we used to rattle off a tune on the old kanoon. Do you know what a kanoon is, little dearie?' Being asked a question she can't answer and being called 'little dearie' in the same breath – both also things that you know she hates – she loses her presence of mind, and forgets the repeat in the Durand.

KATABATIC *a.* In the manner of a downwards-flowing wind which descends into a valley from higher ground. (See *williwaw* for a stronger manifestation of the same phenomenon.) Use, perhaps, to describe a tall person farting.

KEF *n.* A state of voluptuous dreaminess, full of languid contentment. (From the Arabic *kaif*, meaning good humour.) 'No use calling Justin to dinner, Mummy; he's in one of his kefs in the toilet, drooling and giggling at his toothbrush. Which I might say he never seems to use, despite having that old tin full of toothpowder.'

KENNEBUNKER *n.* A large suitcase. 'So Meredith is coming to stay next month, eh? And how many of her kennebunkers will she be bringing this time, do you think?'

KENOGENESIS *n.* A type of biological development in which the characteristics of a particular organism are not typical of those normally possessed by the group to which it belongs. 'Most clerical support officers would be able to spell the word "receive", Barnaby, without any difficulty and without claiming stress leave because of the effort involved. But then ... in your case I suppose a certain allowance must be made for kenogenesis.'

KERCHIEF OF PLEASANCE *phr.* An embroidered cloth worn by a medieval knight in his helmet, or round his arm, in honour of his lady (also sometimes called a favour.) Today's young men could do worse than adopt a similar practice, perhaps obtaining from their girl friend one of her small handkerchiefs, and wearing it proudly in their lapel, their fob pocket, etc.; taking, of course, every opportunity to casually refer to it as 'my kerchief of pleasance'.

KENOSIS *n.* The theological term for Christ's setting aside his divinity to assume human form. 'Oh, all right, if the rest of the family really wants to go and see *Dumb and Dumber*, I suppose as *pater familias* I must accept the necessity of kenosis and join you.'

KERCHIEF OF PLEASANCE *phr.* An embroidered cloth worn by a medieval knight in his helmet, or round his arm, in honour of his lady (also sometimes called a favour.) Today's young men could do worse than adopt a similar practice, perhaps obtaining from their girlfriend one of her small handkerchiefs, and wearing it proudly in their lapel, their fob pocket, etc.; taking, of course, every opportunity to casually refer to it as 'my kerchief of pleasance'.

KILDERKIN *n.* A little barrel or cask, about half the size of a normal wine barrel, containing about nineteen gallons. 'A kilderkin for the road, before we part, Jock? Your turn to pay, I think?'

KINEPHANTOM *n.* An interesting one, this. The technical name for a phenomenon that we have all seen, have all been puzzled by, and have never known the name of. When you are watching a movie or video of a car in motion, and the wheels appear to be going *backwards*, even though you know they must be going forward, you are witnessing a kinephantom.

KINK INSTABILITY *phr.* Once again, I have to say at the outset that I have not made this up. Check in any good science dictionary. The potential for metaphorical uses in home, work and play situations are so evident as not to bear spelling out here. This is a nuclear physics term which describes the bending of plasma, one of the principal forms of instability in plasma. Plasma itself, as every schoolgirl knows, is an ionised gaseous discharge with no resultant charge, since the numbers of positive and negative ions are equal, in addition to unionised molecules or atoms. Do I hear you express doubt about the concept of unionised particles? Then spell it with the hyphen, if you must.

KINNIKINIC *n.* The leaves or bark of certain plants such as the willow when prepared for smoking. 'That? Oh, that's nothing, officer; just a little kinnikinic of my mother's.'

KOBOLD *n.* (From German folklore.) A goblin or gnome who lives underground in caves or mines. Your young brother who spends all his after-school hours locked in the basement with his supposedly secret collections of trading cards and magazines.

KURBASH *n.* A heavy hide whip used as an instrument of torture in former times by the Turks. 'Sorry to hear that crystal therapy hasn't cured your chronic fatigue syndrome, Simon; perhaps a course of the kurbash would do the trick?'

KYRIOLOGIC *a.* Presented in pictorial hieroglyphics form. 'Just essaying a little kyriology,' you proudly say to the person who looks over your shoulder at the doodling in your notebook during the management team meeting.

L

LACHRYMATORY *n.* A little bottle for keeping tears in. Typically a phial of glass or pottery, with a mouth shaped to fit over the eyeball. Sometimes decorated with a picture of an eye. 'And now, viewers, in the face of these allegations, the president is taking out his lachrymatory ... he's putting it to his left eye ... the suspense here is enormous ... yes, he is in fact crying into the lachrymatory!'

LACONIUM *n.* Superior Person's word for a sauna.

LAMELLAR *a.* Made up of thin scales or flakes. Perhaps a polite way to refer to your friend's unfortunate dandruff problem.

LAMIA *n.* A female demon or bloodsucking undead vampire. 'I think Lamia would be a nice name for the Harrisons' new baby, don't you, darling? Why don't you suggest it? They're too suspicious of me now.'

LANUGINOUS *a.* Woolly, covered with down. 'Son, sit down. I'd like to have a word with you. As you grow, certain things happen to your body, and I notice that already your cheeks are becoming lanuginous. That is why your mother and I have decided to present you with this electric razor. Use it wisely.'

LAPPING *n.* The act of privily dropping an object into your lap while seated at a table performing close-up magic. The author not infrequently performs lapping, quite unintentionally, with scrambled eggs – an entirely different effect.

LAPSUS CALAMI *phr.* A slip of the pen. To be distinguished from, but, if at all possible, to be used in close conjunction with, LAPSUS LINGUAE *phr.*, a slip of the tongue, and LAPSUS MEMORIAE *phr.*, a slip of the memory. In short, the Superior Person's way of referring to his own mistakes. Perhaps the famous mistake of Joshua Reynolds, in painting a picture of a man wearing a hat while holding another hat in his hand, could be described as a *lapsus memoriae*. Certainly the mistake made in the so-called 'Wicked Bible' which gives the seventh commandment as 'Thou shalt commit adultery' was a notable *lapsus calami*. But what sort of *lapsus* was Dr Johnson's definition, in his famous dictionary, of 'leeward' as meaning exactly the same as 'windward'? Or the American college-student's assertion in an exam paper that 'Louis Pasteur discovered a cure for rabbis'? The musicologist Nicolas Slonimsky produced a whole book full of mistakes in judgement made by eminent music critics. What sort of *lapsi* are the following? 'There has not been an Italian composer yet more incapable of producing a tune than Verdi.' '*Rigoletto* has hardly any chance of remaining in the repertoire.' 'Tchaikovsky's *First Piano Concerto* is as difficult for popular apprehension as the name of the composer and includes long stretches of what seem a formless void.' 'Chopin effects the crudest modulations; while listening to his music it is hard to form the slightest idea of when wrong notes are played.'

LAPSUS PICTORAE *phr.* An expression invented by the author to fit such errors as the following. Next time you see the famous John Wayne movie *Stagecoach*, which was of course set in the nineteenth century, keep your eyes peeled and at one point you will see tyre tracks in the sand. In *It Happened One Night*, Clark Gable leaves his hotel room at 2.30 a.m., drives around New York, writes a story for his newspaper and returns to his room, where the clock still reads 2.30 a.m. In *The Black Knight*, starring Alan Ladd and, needless to say, set in the Middle Ages, one of the ladies of the court turns her back to the camera and reveals that her dress is secured with a zip fastener. In *The Wrong Box*, set in Victorian times, note how many TV aerials you can see on the roofs of houses.

LARGHISSIMO *adv.* Very slow indeed. The ultimate largo in music. 'If you're really going to try to explain Chinese Checkers to Ryan, take it slow, won't you? His brain works ... how can I put it ... larghissimo?'

LATERITIOUS *a.* Brick-like in colour or general appearance. 'And now a word about the groom. From the day that my daughter first brought Brad to our house, we have always found him to be lateritious to a fault ...'

LATESCENT *a.* Becoming obscure or hidden away, as old-world courtesy in a teenager.

LATIFEROUS *a.* Bearing or containing latex. 'Ah, the latiferous ones approach,' you say, looking out the window at the Halloween trick-or-treaters with their rubber monster masks.

LAZARETTO *n.* A hospital or house for the victims of plague or other quarantinable diseases (originally leprosy). Yes, yet another nice term for your brother's bedroom.

LEMNISCATE *n.* A figure of eight drawn lying on its side. An occult symbol for eternity and the mathematical symbol for infinity. But which infinity? The number of odd numbers or the number of all numbers?

LENTIGINOSE *a.* Freckled. 'Long accustomed to the healthy, open-air life, her beauty is exceeded only by her lentiginosity.'

LEX LOCI *phr.* The law of this place. 'I know that hitting your younger brother over the head with an omelette-maker is consistent with *lex talionis*, Evita, but in this house the *lex loci* prevails, and that explicitly rules out omelette-maker attacks.' (*Lex* *talionis*, of course, is the law of retaliation.)

LIBRATE *v.* To oscillate backwards and forwards before coming to rest. Action of a swinging voter.

LIED *n.* Song. German, and therefore, some think, superior word, but it simply means song, and nothing more. When discussing the *Winterreise* with one of your more pretentious friends, make a point of referring always to the 'songs' which make it up. Ignore the pitying looks. Incidentally, one of the loveliest Schubertian-style lieder known to the author is that by Lord Berners, the distinguished English composer, entitled *Red Roses and Red Noses*. In it, Berners poses the question: which is the better – red roses or red noses? – and comes down in favour of the latter, in the beautiful final lines:

> 'Red noses last a lifetime,
> Red roses but a day.'

LIMINALITY *n.* That part of a *rite de passage* (i.e., an event such as marriage or coronation, marking the transition of a member of society from one state to another) when the moment of transition arrives. 'Father, in the name of liminality I claim the right to join you in your pre-prandial libations.'

LIPOSTOMY *n.* Atrophy of the mouth. Useful term for cursing an overly loquacious sibling: 'May you have lipostomy 'ere nightfall!'

LIXIVIATE *v.* To leach, i.e., to make a liquid percolate through a substance. 'Like me to lixiviate your coffee, Marigold? No? Oh, well, Instant for you, then – percolated for everyone else, eh?'

LOXODROMICS *n.* The art of oblique sailing. They do it deliberately? 'The wharf's out here in front of us, Ashleigh – not over there to the left.' Could be used, perhaps, as a corrective during family driving instruction.

LOXOGONONSPHERICALL *a.* I have no idea what this word means. It is one of the many bizarre neoterisms of Sir Thomas Urquhart, a seventeenth-century cavalier whose fortunes were destroyed by the Revolution and who devoted much of his life to the writing and publication of works reflecting his knowledge of esoteric lore and learning and in particular his highly creative approach to the English language. The word here instanced is from Urquhart's 1644 trigonometrical treatise *Trissotetras*, which is described by the *Encyclopaedia Britannica* as 'impenetrably obscure'. One of the entries in the glossary of this work reads: 'Cathetobasall, is said of the Concordance of Loxogononsphericall Moods, in the Datas of the Perpendicular, and the Base, for finding out of the Maine question'.

LUBRIFACTION *n.* The process of lubricating, or making something slippery. 'Shall we retire to your gynaeceum for a little mutual lubrication, my beloved? After which, who knows?'

LUNATION *n.* The period of time between two reappearances of the new moon. In other words, pretty close to a month; hence the Superior Person's word for that period. 'See you in a couple of lunations, Mason!'

M

MACHICOLATION *n.* An opening at the top of a castle wall through which boiling oil or missiles could be cast down upon a besieging force. The act of so doing.

MACHICOLATE *v.* To construct these openings. 'I see you've had your hair machicolated as well as coloured this time, Kimberley – well done!'

MACKLE *n.* A flaw, stain or blurred impression. In printing, to mackle is to print in such a way as to produce a blurred or double image. When you come across something which has been mackled in the printing, put it aside and get it out later to use as a test piece when your dear old uncle is boasting about his new reading glasses. Speaking of macklish words, one is irresistibly reminded of the old Scottish saying *many a mickle makes a muckle*. I had always assumed this to mean that many small amounts, if combined, make a large amount; but Webster informs me that *mickle* means a large amount and *muckle* means a large quantity. In other words, many large amounts, added together, make a large amount. Come to think of it, a true statement.

MACTATION *n.* The killing of a sacrificial victim. 'In welcoming Dr Fairbrother onto the dais tonight, I want to say that his Office of Meteorological Science can only do so much to help protect us from the ravages of bad weather, of the kind we have all been experiencing lately. The floods may have washed away your crops, your houses, and in many cases dearly beloved family members. But that is not Dr Fairbrother's fault. His office did not make the floods. In any case, I feel sure that after tonight we can all look forward to a brighter future, and after the speeches we will of course be cementing this happy expectation with our age-old ceremony of mactation, in which we will be asking Dr Fairbrother to play the traditional central role.'

MACULATION *n.* Being covered in spots. Condition of a leopard or a teenager.

MAESTOSO *adv.* (In playing music) majestically, nobly. 'Here comes your father, children. Ah, it's his *maestoso* walk tonight! Has he been made a Team Leader at the office? Or has he got a refund on the shirt he bought that was the wrong size?' The use of the standard musical directions for domestic situations has never been fully exploited, and offers all kinds of possibilities. '*Prestissimo, prestissimo!*' when endeavouring to get all three TV-watching children to the dinner table. '*Piano, piano!*' to the same group when you are answering the phone. And so on.

MANDIBULATE *a.* Pertaining to an insect with jaws designed for chewing. Suitable term for one of those continuously gum-chewing sportsmen. Why do they do it?

MANUMIT *v.* To release from servitude, as for example to free a slave. 'Manumission! Manumission!' you cry as your last-born finally leaves home.

MATTOID *a.* Mentally unbalanced with regard solely to a specific subject. 'Wayne and Clark are so sensible in every way; but get them talking about Judy Garland ...'

MEGRIM *n.* Archaic, and therefore Superior Person's, word for migraine.

MENTHACEOUS *a.* To do with the Mentha genus of fragrant perennial herbs of the mint family, including peppermint and spearmint. 'Menthacity is no substitute for sobriety, Nathan. What did you have more of – the martinis or the peppermints?'

MERYCISM *n.* It sometimes falls to the lot of the lexicographer to apprise his readers of strange and fearful things. Merycism is human rumination, a medical condition sufficiently well-established to be dealt with in Gould and Pyle's *Anomalies and Curiosities of Medicine*. Not, of course, rumination in exactly the same sense as applies to cattle and other animals that chew their cud, but *the rechewing of regurgitated food*. A distinguished physiologist, Brown-Séquard, even acquired this habit as a result of experimenting upon himself. Gould and Pyle quote the case of another patient, himself a physician and something of an epicure: 'after a hearty meal the regurgitation was more marked – food had been regurgitated, tasting as good as when first eaten, several hours after the eating'.

MESNE LORD *phr.* (Pronounced 'meany', by the way.) A kind of middle-level person under the feudal system; someone who rents land from a superior lord while himself having a subordinate tenant. 'Daniel, I know that you pay your mother and myself a small token rent for your room, and that we in turn pay rent for the house; and I appreciate your desire to make your college course in medieval studies "come alive", as you so cogently put it; but *must* you always refer to me as your "mesne lord" when talking to your mother?'

METABIOSIS *n.* The dependence of one living organism on another; as for example hairdressers and people with hair, homoeopaths and morons, etc.

METAGNOSTIC *a.* Beyond human understanding. Instructions for Assemble-It-Yourself furniture, the Menu function on your mobile phone, any Help programme in any computer application, the International Date Line, etc.

METASTASIS *n.* Abruptly passing over a subject as though it were insignificant. 'Dad, I wish to raise with you the subject of my borrowing the car tonight. And can we discuss this without the usual metatasis on your part ...'

METEMPIRICISM *n.* The science of pure reason. As exemplified in the General Theory of Relativity, chess endgame theory, code-breaking, etc. For a pleasing example of metempiricism in action, consider this true story about Ramanujau, the self-taught Indian mathematician who was made a fellow of the Royal Society in 1918. Terminally ill in hospital with tuberculosis, he was visited one day by a mathematician friend who, for want of anything better to say, remarked that the number of his taxi, 1729, had seemed a particularly boring one. 'Oh no!' cried Ramanujau at once; 'it is a very interesting number. It is the smallest number expressible as the sum of two cubes in two different ways.'

METOCHY *n.* A zoological term, for the relationship between two different types of living creature that live closely together, tolerating but not helping each other. An example is the cohabitation of certain ants with certain other insects. Or in some cases, I am told, a spouse with a spouse.

MISAPODYSIS *n.* An intense dislike of undressing in front of another person. 'My psychiatrist tells me, Mrs Haberdash, that I need a course of intensive repetitive conditioning therapy to cure me of my misapodysis. This can be done at home in the privacy of a bedroom; but the presence of another person is essential. Could you, perhaps, give up an hour of your time each night to help me with this?'

misapodysis

MISONEISM *n.* A dislike of the new and the changed. Experienced at its most extreme by computer users who have only just mastered the previous disc-operating system when the new one comes out.

MOFETTE *n.* A poisonous release of gas from a hole in the ground; or the hole from which the noxious vapours emerge. 'I just know that Nathan's smoking in the basement again! And why those awful Ethiopian cigars, instead of cannabis like a normal person! Talk about your ultimate mofette!'

MOKADOR *n.* A napkin or handkerchief, more especially for tucking into the collar to receive food droppings. In short, a bib. 'Scrambled eggs this morning – better get out your mokador, darling!'

MONOPLEGIA *n.* Impressive medical name for writer's cramp. Overtaken, now that the pen has been replaced by the computer, by osteoarthritis of the small joints – especially if, like most authors, you use only two fingers.

MOROLOGY *n.* In speech or writing, being deliberately

foolish or nonsensical as a means of achieving a
desired effect. A technique not often employed by
the present author, who ordinarily makes his effects
by being *accidentally* foolish or nonsensical.

MOZETTA *n.* A kind of cowled coat worn by prelates in
the Catholic Church. 'One thing I always say – it's
not a proper pizza without mozetta.'

MUCOPURULENT *a.* Containing a mixture of mucus and
pus. Exceptionally useful epithet for vituperative
purposes.

MUSOPHOBIA *n.* The morbid dread of mice. Supposedly
a condition of the female human, though not of any
female known to the present author.

MUSQUASH *n.* A muskrat. 'So, you're a vegetarian,
Bronwyn? Perhaps, then, you'd like a little
musquash with your pumpkin?'

mysophobia

MYSOPHOBIA *n.* The morbid dread of contamination,
e.g., from contact with dirt. 'We simply must have a
heart-to-heart talk with Amphibia. Being a little

fastidious about entering Liam's room is one thing; but this thing she has about spraying all of us with bleach aerosol whenever she comes into the family room – it's mysophobia gone mad.'

MYTHOMANIA *n.* Pathological and continued lying in which the person concerned actually believes his or her own lies. It is thought that many cult leaders, politicians and alternative healing practitioners reach this stage of affliction.

MYTHOPOEIA *n.* The deliberate and knowing creation of myth. 'Well, we've heard your account of what happened at the office Christmas party. So much for the mythopoeia. Now – let's have the real story!'

N

NACKET *n.* Superior Person's word for a tennis ball-boy.

NARAPOIA *n.* A mental illness in which the sufferer believes that he is following someone, and that people are out to do him good. The credit for this delightful *neoterism* (q.v.) does not rest with this lexicographer, but with a science-fiction writer whose name, alas, I can no longer recall.

NECRENCEPHALUS *n.* Softening of the brain. Superior insult word.

NEOPHOBIA *n.* The morbid dread of anything new. The nineteenth-century writer Samuel Rogers once said that whenever a new book came out, he made a point of reading an old one. A sentiment shared by the present author. When *Angela's Ashes* came out, I at once read *The Tenant of Wildfell Hall*.

NEOTERISM *n.* That which is new, and especially the invention of new words, or a particular newly coined word (the latter being also known as a *neologism*). For example, when Sir Thomas Urquhart (see *loxogononsphericall*) published his translation of Rabelais, he enriched the text by expanding a list of nine animal sounds to seventy-one, including the curking of quails, the nuzzing of camels, the smuttering of monkeys, the charming of beagles, the drintling of turkeys, the boing of buffaloes, the coniating of storks, the gueriating of apes, and the crouting of cormorants.

noctambulation

NEPHANALYSIS *n.* The analysis of cloud patterns. 'One day, Sis, you must do some nephanalysis on that stuff you spray on your hair; might be something in there to control the Bronze Orange Bug.'

NIMBUS *n.* In ancient art, a disc or plate, often golden, sometimes multi-coloured, placed vertically behind the head of a person of special sanctity or dignity, as a badge, so to speak, of honour. The *halo*, which is normally a ring hovering horizontally over the head but may also take the form of a general radiance around the head, carries a similar significance. As does the *gloriole*, i.e., the circle of light around the head of pictured saints. Originally a symbol of power in the pre-Christian world, the nimbus was widely adopted in Christian art in the Middle Ages. When the rest of the family are seated at the dinner table, try making an entrance while holding one of your wife's best decorated china plates behind your head, so that, when questioned, you can explain that this is your nimbus. If not questioned, of course, your little jape will have failed embarrassingly, and all you can then resort to is a feeble: 'Well, who's for a game of *nurspell* (q.v.)?'

NIPHABLEPSIA *n.* Snow blindness. 'Oh, the niphablepsia! The niphablepsia! I know confirmation dresses are supposed to be white, but . . . I'm blinded! I'm blinded! I don't think I'll be able to go to the service!'

NOBILIARY PARTICLE *phr.* One of those prefixes such as *de* or *von* which, before a personal name, indicate noble ancestry. Remarkably useful to add to one's name when making a booking at a London hotel. In his book *The Rights of Man*, Tom Paine referred to the nobility as the 'No Ability'.

NOCTAMBULATION *n.* Superior person's word for sleepwalking, otherwise known as somnambulism. The latter being a wonderful item for spelling tests, by the way; the first *m* gets them every time, possibly because of the wide currency of the Italian form *sonnambula* in the title of Bellini's opera.

NOCTIFLOROUS *a.* Blooming at night. 'We just have to face the fact that our daughter is noctiflorous. We'll have to try for the family Christmas photo in the window of opportunity between her leaving her bedroom tonight and getting out the front door.'

NOLENS VOLENS *phr.* Latin phrase meaning 'whether unwilling or willing', and of course the origin of the common English phrase 'willy-nilly', the oddity being that in the latter case the two components of the phrase are mutually transposed. So, in future when expressing this concept, don't say 'willy-nilly'; say 'nilly-willy'. This will confirm your reputation as a tiresome eccentric and at the same time enable you to correct your well-meaning correctors.

NOMOLOGY *n.* The study of laws and lawmaking. Also that branch of any specific discipline which deals with its laws, e.g., the nomology of physics. But what is the nomology of nomology called?

NOSTOLOGY *n.* The study of second childhood in extreme old age. 'Mum, do you know what Dad's doing? He's been buying all these comics, and I caught him writing away for a skull ring and a pair of Magic X-Ray Spectacles! And he keeps saying he's a nostologist!'

NOSTOMANIA *n.* An unduly powerful or excessive nostalgia. 'Nostalgia ain't what it used to be; it used to be nostomania.'

NOSTOPATHY *n.* A morbid dread of returning to one's home. A more useful contribution to philology would perhaps be a word for a morbid dread of someone else returning to one's home.

NOUMENON *n.* The transcendent, unknowable, mystical essence of something, in contradistinction to the *phenomenon*, an objective entity which may be directly perceived by the senses. Walk into your teenager's poster-bedecked bedroom when he or she is out and empty your mind of all other thoughts for a moment, and you may gain some idea of the concept.

NOVERCAL *a.* In the manner of a stepmother. 'Mother, I think you're perfectly beastly about this curfew thing. Just because you can't relate to Luke's innovative body-piercing. You're just so ... so *novercal*!'

NULLIFIDIAN *a.* or *n.* Without religious faith; one who is without religious faith. Useful when confronted by religious proselytisers at your front door. If you admit to them that you are an agnostic or an atheist, they will merely redouble their efforts to convert you; but a smiling statement that you are a nullifidian will send them away content, if somewhat baffled.

NUMEN *n.* An internal spirit or power that gives life and/or guidance. 'Leave your father alone for a few minutes, you children – can't you see that his numen is weakening?'

NUMMULAR *a.* Coin-shaped; pertaining to the possession of money. Given two meanings, on being introduced to your daughter's latest hopeful, you might say to your wife, 'Well, he's certainly nummular – but is he nummular?'

NUNCUPATIVE *a.* In legal matters, oral rather than written. (Be it noted, by the way, that 'verbal' is not the same as 'oral'. All language, whether oral or written, is verbal.) 'Yes, I do seem to recall saying something about a substantial monetary reward if you got straight *A*'s this term; but, Leonard, we're talking a nuncupative undertaking here, I think, aren't we? And you know what that means?'

NURSPELL *n.* I give here the scholarly J. W. Mollet's definition of *nurspell* in full: 'An old English game like trap, bat and ball. It is played with a kibble, a nur and a spell. When the end of the spell is struck with the kibble, the nur rises in the air, etc.' *Etcetera*? What is this etcetera? This man should be writing instructions for changing computer settings.

NYCTOPHOBIA *n.* The morbid dread of night. Question: would it be possible for a nyctophobic to suffer also from *photophobia* (q.v.)? Think about it.

NYMPHAEUM *n.* A nymph's shrine. Today, a daughter's unguent-bestrewn dressing table.

O

OBDORMITION *n.* The technical term for that familiar physical condition – the 'going to sleep' of a limb when pressure on a nerve has caused a tingly numbness. 'Waldemar is the only person I know who gets obdormition of the brain.'

OBEX *n.* Any device that can hold a door shut, such as a lock, a latch, a bolt or a crossbar. 'I don't care how much it costs; if Daryl is going to be alone in the house after school, I want an obex for the door of my room.'

OBLATION *n.* In canon law (see *canonical age*), any property that is given to the church. Oddly, there seems to be no word for property given by the church, as for example to the poor. In Shaw's play *Captain Brasshound's Conversion*, one of the characters expresses alarm at being in a Moslem country, saying that Moslems believe that they will go to heaven if they kill a Christian. 'Don't worry,' replies another character, 'in England the people are

Christians, and believe that they will go to heaven if they give their money to the poor – but they don't do it!'

OBNUBILATION *n.* A state of consciousness in which the mind is clouded over and the thinking processes vague. 'I know it's only just after breakfast, darling, and we can't expect obnubilation to have entirely dissipated yet, but do you really think you should be going to the office wearing your pyjama pants under your designer slacks?'

OMNIPHAGOUS *a.* Eating everything. One of the great experimental omniphages was William Buckland, the first Professor of Geology at Oxford University. He ate hedgehog, crocodile and mole meat, and even a blue-bottle fly, the taste of which he considered the most repulsive he had ever experienced. Once when lost on a dark night during a ride to London with a friend, he dismounted, scooped up a handful of earth, smelt it, and immediately declared: 'Uxbridge!' The Archbishop of York once proudly showed Buckland a snuff box containing the heart of Louis XIV, which the Archbishop had bought from a tomb-robber when in Paris during the revolution. Remarking, 'I've eaten many things, but never the heart of a king,' Buckland seized the heart and swallowed it on the spot.

ophidiophobia

OPHELIMITY *n.* The ability to give sexual pleasure. (See *orexigenic*.)

OPHIDIOPHOBIA *n.* The morbid dread of snakes. As distinct from the ordinary common-or-garden dread of snakes – particularly in the common or garden.

OREXIGENIC *a.* Whetting the appetite, especially the sexual appetite. 'Morning, Miss Wesley,' you say as you pass her desk; 'orexigenic *and* ophelimitous this morning, I see!' You are quite safe. She will be able to find neither of these two words in the *Secretary's Handy Desk Dictionary*.

ORISMOLOGY *n.* The explanation of technical terms. Such as orismology.

ORNAMENTS RUBRIC *phr.* A rubric (i.e., a direction for the performance of divine worship, originally printed in red) relating to the vestments which the officiating ministers should wear. 'Finlay, you know perfectly well that when we visit Aunt Martha, the ornaments rubric for the day specifically prohibits the wearing of a T-shirt embroidered with the slogan "Shit happens".'

OROGRAPHY *n.* In physical geography, the study of mountains and mountain systems. As you pack the ski gear into your friend's car, you assure your mother that this is for your compulsory unit in Orography III.

ORTHOGRAPHY *n.* Spelling correctly. The great nineteenth-century critic Saint-Beuve once offended a journalist, who immediately challenged him to a duel. Saint-Beuve accepted the challenge, saying: 'As the challenged party, I have the right to choose weapons. I choose spelling – you're dead!'

OSCITANCY *n.* The act of yawning, or a state of exceptional drowsiness. 'Ladies and gentlemen, our guest lecturer tonight will be talking about "Great Moments in the History of Accrual Accounting". Prepare yourselves for an evening of pure oscitancy!'

OSMOPHOBIA *n.* A morbid dread of odours. Such as those generated by a sufferer from *osmidrosis* (strong-smelling perspiration), especially if the osmophobe also has *osmethesia* (a strong sensitivity to odours).

OSTINATO *n.* A musical term used to describe a repetitive and simple melodic theme which serves as an underpinning for the main line of music, as in the example of an ostinato bass. From the Latin word for obstinate. 'Thank you for taking little Bobbie on the school excursion today, Mr Pomfrey. I know it's a long trip, but you'll find his singing away, there in the back seat, a charming accompaniment to the journey, I just know. His current favourite is "Baa baa black sheep" – he loves it so much, he just won't stop. But you play whatever you want to on the radio, of course. He'll just provide the ostinato background.'

OUPHE *n.* (Pronounced 'oof'.) An elf, gnome or goblin. 'Yes, Director, this is our kindergarten class, and here are all our little ouphes sitting at their little tables cutting out their little pieces of coloured paper. Would you like them to sing to you?'

OUTSERT *n.* I love this word. A genuine printing term, meaning a folded sheet of printed paper which is wrapped *around the outside of* another folded section. In other words, the opposite of *insert*.

OVIPOSIT *v.* To lay an egg. 'Hope the new book oviposits well and truly!' is your encouraging remark to the new author.

P

PALANQUIN *n.* A covered litter in which persons of importance were transported from place to place, borne by poles resting on the shoulders of two or four men. Given the height above road level at which the passenger sat, the nearest modern analogy is probably one of those urban four-wheel-drive vehicles which sit alongside you at the traffic lights, blocking your view of the entire street. The analogy breaks down, however, when one considers the relative importance of the persons thus conveyed.

PALINGENESIS *n.* A new or second birth into a higher form of being. Not quite the same as *resurrection*, but close enough to enable you to introduce a nice element of confusion into any theological discussion. The greatest claim to fame of the post-war American pentecostalist preacher William Branham was his resurrection of a fish. *Pentecost* itself is an interesting word, referring as it does to both Jewish and Christian festivals as well as to extremes of fundamentalist behaviour. And did you know that a *pentecostys* was a division of fifty Spartan soldiers?

PALIURUS *n.* A Mediterranean thorny bush, with long, sharp spikes, sometimes called 'Christ's thorn' because it is said to have been used to make the crown of thorns that was placed upon the head of Jesus. 'Well done, Jaclyn, well done! Second place in the class spelling competition! Now let the orthographer be crowned with a wreath of paliurus!'

PEASCOD-BELLY *n.* A false stomach worn under the clothing by Elizabethan men as part of the then fashionable use of sculpted underwear to convey an artificial impression of an exaggerated body shape. The peascod-belly was made by stuffing a whalebone or wooden frame with old rags, sawdust, bran, etc. There is an account of one unfortunate gallant whose peascod-belly caught on a nail as he was ceremonially advancing to make his obeisances to Queen Elizabeth, with the result that its filling escaped and left him deflated literally as well as metaphorically in front of the whole court. Today, the concept of the peascod-belly can perhaps be used as part of a response to any unkind reference to your 'beer-belly'. Simply convert your unfortunate affliction into a fashion statement.

PERIPETY *n.* A sudden and dramatic reversal of fortune – normally from good to bad. 'Ashleigh has chosen voluntary redundancy, from the limited choices available to him, and in making this farewell speech I know that those of you who have worked with him for so long, and, ha, ha, enjoyed – for want of a better word – his unique management style, will join with me in wishing him complete peripety from this point on.'

PERISTASIS *n.* The complete environment of a living organism, including all the procesess vital to its life. 'This really is your peristatis, isn't it?' you enquire wearily of your teenage son as he reclines on the couch before his array of digital audio and video pleasure machines.

PETALIFEROUS *a.* Having petals. 'Nice dress – so petaliferous.'

PHATIC *a.* Denoting speech which consists of noises rather than words, i.e., when emotions rather than thoughts are being communicated, as for example in baby talk or when a cat owner is engaged in a miaowing dialogue with her cat. Sometimes also called 'idiot salutations'. Mode of communication much favoured by grandparents.

PHILOGYNY *n.* The love of, indeed devotion to, women. The most understandable of idiosyncrasies.

PHONOMANIA *n.* Homicidal mania. One of those words that could be thought to mean anything but what it really means. Something to say when you are interrupted at dinner by a telemarketer selling a new phone-billing offer. 'Ah, you're giving me a real case of phonomania! Why not give me your name and private address, and I'll call round one night!'

PHOTODRAMA and **PHOTOPLAY** *n.* Both words simply mean a motion picture, and were in common use in the early days of the kinematograph. Remarks such as 'Well, we went along to the cinema yesterday and saw a wonderful photodrama, starring an actor named Alberto Pacino,' will reinforce your reputation as a lovable eccentric.

PHOTOPHOBIA *n.* The morbid dread of light. You know – that thing of Dracula's. And of the computer generation.

photophobia

PIAFFER *n.* In the art of formal or ceremonial horse-riding for display purposes, a piaffer is a particular movement in which the horse is made to lift a forefoot and the diagonally opposite hindfoot at the same time and then slowly place them forwards, backwards or to one side. Humans do this, though less gracefully, and call it line dancing. The Hubble telescope has searched to the furthest reaches of the known universe and has, I understand, failed to find a more boring form of animate activity than line dancing, so when next you find yourself a stupefied spectator as groups of strangely clad people prepare to lift their cowboy-booted feet in the closest to unison that they can manage, wait for a moment's silence and then call out, with feigned enthusiasm, in a loud voice: 'With a hey nonny nonny and a hot cha cha! Let the piaffering begin!'

PILLIWINKS *n.* The thumbscrews. 'OK,' you cry, after being compelled to play Scrabble so many times in succession that your host has at last succeeded in winning a round, 'now let's have some real fun! Who's for pilliwinks?'

PIMPERNEL *n.* For those of you who have always wanted to know what the famous 'scarlet pimpernel' really is: a plant of the primrose family.

PISHOGUE *n.* A yellowish-white fungus, thought to be made at dead of night by a group of malevolent men and women, after a solemn invocation of the devil, as a means of cursing a rival dairyfarmer's produce. A practice, and belief, still extant in the twenty-first century. This certainly explains the condition of the can of evaporated milk left opened and forgotten at the back of the refrigerator.

PISTOLOGY *n.* The study of faith. Presumably it was as an exercise in pistology that the BBC recently questioned 103 English bishops, and discovered that only three believed in the biblical version of the creation of the world, eighty doubted the story of

Adam and Eve, and one in four did not believe that Jesus was born of a virgin.

PLASTRON *n.* A decorative addition to the front of a woman's dress, reaching from the waist upwards to the throat, or as near to it as the dress allows. Also a fencer's leather breastplate, and the bottom side of a turtle's protective shell. Similarly, a *plastrum* is the starched front of a man's evening shirt, or an iron breastplate in medieval armour. 'Would you mind putting your hand up my plastrum, Miss Lackenby, to straighten it out for me?'

PLEIOSYLLABIC *a.* Having more than one syllable (more especially, having two or three). 'Definitely not a pleiosyllabicist!' is perhaps the safest comment you can make when asked your opinion of your sister-in-law's latest reflexologist.

PLURISIGNATION *n.* Multiple meanings simultaneously expressed in poetic language (as distinct from ambiguity, which implies a choice of alternative meanings). A worthy end, to which this book, one earnestly hopes, is a means.

PLUVIOMETER *n.* Superior person's word for a rain gauge. See also UDOMETER.

PORSONIAN *a.* An unashamed *neoterism* (q.v.) on the part of the author, referring to excessive indulgence in the cup that cheers. After Dr Richard Porson (1759–1808), the greatest classical scholar in the age of classical scholarship, and a drunkard on a truly heroic scale. According to the historian Timbs,

Porson was 'scarcely more ahead of his contemporaries in Greek than he was in drinking, in which his excesses were frightful'. He would drink anything, including ink, liniment and, once, in mistake for gin, a bottle of lamp oil.

POSTULANT *n.* One who seeks admission to a religious order. 'So – be it known that Mum and Dad seek admission to our game of Trivial Pursuit. Are the postulants ready to avow that they will not lose their temper when soundly beaten; that they will not seek to be reminded of the rules and procedure on more than five occasions per half-hour; that they will not, on being informed that they have given an incorrect answer, use the words "I don't think that's right"; and that they will not exclaim, at the end of the game, "I don't know how anyone can be expected to know those questions – I've never heard of those pop singers!" They are? Then let the postulants be admitted.'

POTOMANIA *n.* Alcoholism, dipsomania, delirium tremens – three somewhat different things, be it noted, the word therefore raising the possibility that all three conditions could be experienced at the same time. (See *porsonian*.)

PRESTIDIGITATION *n.* Sleight of hand. Literally, 'quick fingering'. 'My magic skills are getting better, Desirée; how about coming into my room for a little prestidigitation?'

PROEM *n.* A prolegomenon, prolusion, prelude, introduction, foreword, or exordium.

PROTOHUMAN *n.* or *a.* A primitive form of hominid, pre-dating homo sapiens. 'Well, Shannon's taste in boyfriends is improving. This latest primate of hers may be protohuman, but at least he's hominid.'

PRUNELLA *n.* A woollen cloth used both as a dress fabric and for the uppers of shoes. Also, a shoe made with prunella. Also of course a person's name, thereby providing a unique opportunity for wordplay in the event of such a person coming your way.

PSILOSIS *n.* Two different meanings: alopecia (i.e., baldness) and sprue (a tropical disease). In cursing an enemy, your imprecation could therefore include, as the climactic phrase, 'and *both* kinds of psilosis'.

PSITTACISM *n.* A string of meaningless, repetitive words. Literally 'parrot talk'. Superior person's word for New Age mantras and grandparental phaticisms. (See *phatic*.)

PUSTULANT *a.* or *n.* Causing pustules to appear; or a pharmaceutical that causes pustules to appear. 'And now, a little pustulant for Matthew?' you enquire avuncularly, as you offer the little chap a piece of chocolate.

PYRIFORM *a.* Shaped like a pear. But what *is* shaped like a pear – other than, of course, a pear?

PYROTIC *a.* Corrosive. 'No, the punch is non-alcoholic, I assure you. Jennifer has just put a little pyrotic in it, to stimulate the taste buds – that's all.'

Q

QUADRIVIUM *n.* Everyone knows that in medieval times the seven liberal arts that composed the curriculum of educational institutions were divided into the four more advanced subjects (the quadrivium) and the three lesser subjects (the trivium). But how many of you can name the seven subjects? Or the seven wonders of the ancient world, for that matter? The quadrivium was made up of Arithmetic, Geometry, Astronomy and Music; the trivium of Grammar, Logic and Rhetoric. In the modern curriculum, Grammar, Logic and Rhetoric have been replaced by Sports Studies, Media Appreciation, and Self-actualisation, thus giving the term 'trivium' a renewed level of significance.

QUADRUMANE *a.* Having four prehensile hands or feet, like a monkey. A muttered 'Quadrumane!' is a satisfyingly ladylike parting shot at your young brother as he leaves the room after an argument.

QUADRUPLICITIES *n.* One of the many quaint terms

used by astrologers, this refers to the grouping of the twelve signs of the zodiac into three groups of four: the cardinal (Aries, Libra, Cancer and Capricorn), the fixed (Taurus, Scorpio, Leo and Aquarius), and the mutable (Gemini, Sagittarius, Virgo and Pisces). Tell someone that you are aware of their quadruplicity; this is guaranteed to leave them vaguely unsettled.

QUIETIST *n.* One who practises quietism – that is to say, the doctrine that true exaltation of the spirit is attained only by self-denial and passive contemplation. When the fundamentalists call to discuss your belief in God and the coming Armageddon, just put your finger to your lips and hold up a simply lettered cardboard sign reading WE ARE QUIETISTS. Then smile benignly and close the door.

QUIETUS *n.* A blow or other action bringing about death; a *coup de grâce*. As in *Hamlet*: 'his quietus make / With a bare bodkin ...' (a bodkin being a pin or other pointed instrument such as stiletto). A suggestively gentle word for a grim thing. 'Time for your quietus now, children,' you gently say, as you usher your visitors' uncontrolled little offspring out of the lounge room; 'I have some lovely plastic bags for you to play with in the rumpus room.'

QUINTAIN *n.* Something set in place to be tilted at. 'I don't know why you children have to keep pestering me while I'm cooking. There's your father out there on the sun lounger – let him be your quintain instead!'

QUIRT *n.* A braided leather riding whip with a short handle. 'A taste of the quirt, Leonie?' you politely enquire, offering her the hors d'oeuvres.

QUOTHA! *excl.* (Pronounced 'quoather', by the way). Exclamation indicative of surprise, with a slight overlay of derision. Much the same effect as 'Forsooth!' 'I came all the way from town by the mountain route, and the old car used one quart of petrol!' 'Quotha!'

quirt

R

RAMENTUM *n.* (Plural *ramenta*.) A tiny flake that has been rubbed or scraped off something. 'Mummy, it's disgusting! Luke has left his ramenta all over the vanity unit again! I want my own bathroom like you and Daddy have!'

RAREE SHOW *phr.* A lovely old-fashioned phrase which should be used more often than it is. A raree show was a travelling showman's cheap little peepshow or bizarre exhibit, typically but not always carried in a box. When your daughter's new boyfriend, during his first dinner with the family, has finished showing off his skills of catching a pile of coins from his elbow, catching thrown peanuts in his mouth, turning both eyeballs inwards and cracking his knuckles at will, you could clap your hands with simulated delight and thank your daughter for having brought such a raree show into the home.

RATIOCINATE, RATIOCINANT *a.* It's important to get these right. Oh, all right, it's not really. But it's knowledge that only you will have. Used as an adjective, ratiocinate means 'reasoned about', whereas ratiocinant means 'reasoning'. Thus: 'Our business plan was ratiocinate enough, God knows, but unfortunately the ratiocinant beings who developed it were not very good at ratiocination.'

RAVEL *v.* No, not the composer's name. One of those few words which means exactly the same as its apparent opposite. (*Flammable* means the same as *inflammable*; *boned* means the same as *deboned*.) Believe it or not, to ravel something is to unravel it. 'Ravel the morning paper for me, will you, dear?'

RECUBATION *n.* Reclining in a near-horizontal position, as did ancient Romans at the banquet table. 'There'll be no recubation at *this* dinner table, young man! Sit up straight – and take off that baseball cap!'

REPLEVIN *n.* A legal term, denoting an inquiry the purpose of which is to restore to an owner goods that have been wrongfully taken away from him. As a literary term it refers to an inquiry intended to achieve a deserved reputation for a writer hitherto denied recognition. Join the Peter Bowler Replevin movement now! Send your petitions to booksellers everywhere!

RESISTENTIALISM *n.* A fictitious philosophical system, created by Paul Jennings in the late 1940s, to account for the apparent harassment by inanimate matter of human beings. As for example in the failure of the car to start on the one occasion when it is vital that it does, or the jamming open of the zip on your fly just when you are about to return from the toilet to the dais to give your speech at the convention. This raises the attractive possibility of creating other fictitious philosophical systems for domestic use. 'Sorry, darling, but your proposal that we break our trip here to spend time in the Craftie Haven Hand-Painted Rusticware Centre is precluded by my long-held Resistentialism; we must press on without delay!'

replevin

RETICULUM *n.* Any net-like structure. Well, what could be more net-like than a net? 'Ashleigh, you check the height of the reticulum while I go and get a *nacket* (q.v.). And who's brought the tennis balls?'

RETROCESSION *n.* Retreat; returning a property to a former owner; and (of a disease) turning inwards into the body as distinct from breaking out, e.g., through the skin. The general sense is one of *extremity* of retreat. 'Have you seen Mum's face?

Let's be there to watch when Dad comes in, and see how long it takes him to go into retrocession mode.'

RETROCOGNITION *n.* A form of extra-sensory perception in which the clairvoyant becomes aware of something that has happened in the past without having been told about it. 'Matthew, I feel an act of retrocognition coming on! You enter the room having been out all morning – and without having any empirical evidence to tell me this, I suddenly feel that I know with absolute certainty that you have spent the entire morning playing computer games at the mall!'

REVETMENT *n.* A sloping structure, of masonry, timber, etc., intended to act as a retaining wall to support a terrace, the bank of a river, the side of a railway cutting, or other swelling protuberance. 'Ah, Mrs Zaftig, how I admire your revetment!'

RHYNCHOCEPHALIAN *a.* Pertaining to an almost-extinct order of lizardlike reptiles. The implication of this dictionary definition is that the creature in question is not a lizard, merely *like* a lizard. In that case, what is it? In any case, suitable as a descriptor for any of your acquaintances who are lizardlike and reptilian.

RITORNELLO *n.* In music (or for that matter poetry), a short sequence that is repeated like a refrain. Literally, 'little return', thus opening up the possibility of truth in investment advertising: 'Invest your money in our private scheme for Internet options futures! Ritornello!!'

ROBUR *n.* In ancient Roman times, a subterranean dungeon within a prison, used as a place of execution for criminals. Also called a *carnificina*. 'To the robur within you!' you cry, pointing down the steps to the basement.

ROGATION *n.* A supplication to God; a prayer in which a specific request is made of the Deity. (From the ancient Roman term for the submission of a proposed new law to the people.) Sir Francis Galton, the great nineteenth-century scientist who invented fingerprints and eugenics, once carried out a statistical survey of the proportion of prayers which were answered. Another of his surveys was of the geographical distribution of good looks in Britain. (He found that the prettiest women were in London and the ugliest in Aberdeen.) Galton wore his own Universal Patent Ventilating Hat, a top hat with a crown which could be raised by the action of a tube and a squeezable rubber bulb, thereby allowing the overheated head to cool.

ROMERIA *n.* A festival held at a local shrine. 'Don't give me that stuff about obligatory attendance at a romeria! I know you're just going down to the bar to drink with your golf cronies!'

ROTURIER *n.* Someone without any rank or status in society. A peasant, a plebeian, a day-labourer, a schoolteacher or a civil servant.

RUFOUS *a.* Coloured a dullish red or rusty reddish-brown. Reserve the term strictly for use in circumstances where someone named Rufus has just come in from working in the garden. Be patient. At least once in your life, this will happen.

S

SABIANISM *n.* The worship of heavenly bodies. Would the Miss World and Miss Universe competitions attract a little less opprobrium, perhaps, if they were to register as religious organisations, and call their adherents sabians?

SCIOPHILOUS *a.* (Of plants) shade-loving; thriving in shady conditions. The plants that you and I always plant in full sun.

SCRIPTORIUM *n.* The room in a monastery where books are written and copied. Superior Person's word for a study.

SKEUOMORPH *n.* An archaeological term to describe an object which has been made in such a way as to look like a similar one made in a different material; for example, a ceramic pot shaped and coloured to look like a bronze one. In today's households, a number of plastic articles, synthetic busts, etc. might be so described. 'So you've visited the Jarrods at last, eh?

It's skeuomorph heaven in there, isn't it?'

SLUMGULLION *n.* A stew made out of meat and vegetables. But also, be it noted, one of those wonderful words with a range of alternative meanings, all of them pejorative: a menial servant; a weak drink; fish offal; bluffer refuse; and the gunk at the bottom of mine sluiceways. "Heavens, no, Bentley; in calling you a slumgullion I certainly didn't mean to imply that you were a cheap plate of food; look up the other meanings in a dictionary – I think you'll be pleasantly surprised.'

SOLMIZATION *n.* Using what would otherwise be nonsense syllables for the notes in the musical scale. Otherwise known as *solfeggio*: do, re, mi, fa, etc. 'You ask what I think of Lucille's singing, Mrs Weatherpost? Well, I honestly think she's reached the point where she could progress to solmization now.'

SOMNIFACIENT *a.* Conducive to the onset of sleep; having a hypnotic effect. Also *somniferous*, a slightly stronger expression of the same sense, meaning sleep-inducing or narcotic. A televised golf tournament, a line-dancing display in the mall, white-goods comparison shopping, etc., etc.

SPATIOTEMPORAL *a.* Having both space and time. 'Do we really need to invite the Harbingers? I mean – it's a small room, they're so big and so boring – so kind of . . . spatiotemporal.'

SPIRITUAL WIFE *phr.* According to Mormon tradition, my sources claim, a woman who has been married for eternity. In fact it only seems like that to her.

SPOONERISM *n.* We all know that this term describes the kind of metathesis (verbal reversals involving the transposition of initial letters or half-syllables) associated with the name of the Reverend William Spooner (1844–1930). But in fact most of the spoonerisms conventionally attributed to him ('our queer old Dean' instead of 'our dear old Queen' and so on) were never actually said by Spooner. One that is reliably recorded as a true Spoonerism occurred when he was leading prayers at New College, Oxford, and began by saying, 'Darken our lightness, we beseech Thee, O Lord'. Similar errors can appear in print, and the publisher Kegan Paul, in his autobiography, admits to one that slipped past his proof-readers: a wild rock-strewn coastal plain, described by the author as being 'scattered with erratic blocks', came out in print as being 'scattered with erotic blacks'.

STATISTICIAN *n.* As every schoolboy and several schoolgirls knows and know respectively, Dr Johnson defined a lexicographer as 'a harmless drudge', leading the present lexicographer naturally to the suggestion that a statistician be defined as 'a harmless drudge with an understanding of mathematical probability'. Be that as it may, the paradigm of the type is perhaps Charles Babbage, the nineteenth-century inventor of the calculating engine, who once took the trouble to write to the poet Alfred, Lord Tennyson about one of the poet's lines that had been troubling him. Tennyson had written this couplet:

'Every moment dies a man
Every moment one is born.'
Babbage, in his letter to Tennyson, said: 'it must be manifest that if this were true, the population of the world would be at a standstill', and suggested to Tennyson that he revise the lines to read:

'Every moment dies a man
Every moment one and one sixteenth is born.'
Speaking of Alfred, Lord Tennyson, by the way, the author wishes to state that in future he chooses to be known as Peter, Lord Bowler.

STICHOMYTHIA *n.* A form of dialogue in which two speakers engage in a kind of verbal duel, each repeating part of what the previous speaker has said, but in a different sense. The example most frequently quoted is Hamlet's 'Mother, you have my father much offended', in reply to the Queen's 'Hamlet, you have thy father much offended'. A somewhat better-known example, which protracts the conceit to unendurable length, is Abbott and Costello's 'Who's On First' routine.

STOCHASTIC *a.* Unpredictable in progression. In physics and probability theory, a stochastic process is a progression in which the next step cannot be predicted from the preceding steps. 'Oh look – Daddy's coming home at last, Mummy. He's getting out of the taxi ... he's straightening up ... he's putting the bottle away in his pocket ... he's turning towards the house ... now let the stochastic process commence.'

STREPHOSYMBOLIA *n.* A neurological disorder

affecting the ability to read, in which a book may need to be read upside down to be understood. The author had already formed the opinion that some books are better read upside down; and the novels of Dashiell Hammett, he finds, can be enjoyed as much by reading the chapters in backwards as in forward order.

STROBILATION *n.* Reproduction without sexual congress, as for example in jellyfish and tapeworms. 'How do you think Gerald came into existence? Strobilation? I mean – can you imagine Agnes and Simon actually . . . you know . . .?'

SUCCENTOR *n.* One who assists a precentor (a church choir leader). At the high school where you teach, when the pubescent Rochelle proudly informs you that she has been chosen as a cheerleader for the football season, you ask her, with your most irritatingly paternalistic smile, 'Will they take you on as a succentor first and then you work your way up to precentor?'; and, when she asks you what you mean, you tell her to ask her classics teacher (knowing full well that the school has not had a classics teacher since 1923).

SUCCINCTORIUM *n.* An embroidered band of cloth, worn hanging from the girdle by the Pope on solemn occasions. (Passing thought: what occasions involving the Pope are *not* solemn?) The Catholics' reply to the sporran. Unsettle your Scottish friend when he appears, bare-kneed but otherwise expensively clad for the big occasion, with a quiet query about his succinctorium hanging perhaps an inch or so too low?

SUSTENTACULAR *a.* Supporting or maintaining. (From the Latin *sustentare*, to hold up.) 'Ah, Mrs Zaftig, we meet again! Goodness me, your revetment is indeed sustentacular today!'

SYNTONY *n.* The tuning of a specific transmitter and receiver into harmony with each other. Thus, syntonise: to put two pieces of wireless equipment into mutual resonance. 'Now that we're engaged, darling, do you think that before the marriage we should make sure that we can syntonise? It's a simple procedure that takes only a few minutes. We could do that now if you wanted to, right here in your bedroom.'

T

TABULA RASA *phr.* A clean slate. Commonly used metaphorically to describe the mind of a baby as being in effect a blank upon which the experiences of life will be imprinted over the years. Of course, you could also use it to describe the mind of a certain rather older person of your acquaintance; there'll be someone you know who fits the bill.

tabula rasa

TALARIA *n.* One of those wonderful words, like *caduceus* (look it up!), which denote a specific object seen relatively often in illustrations but maddeningly unnameable. The talaria are those little wings that you see on the feet or ankles of the fleet-footed messenger God Mercury (and sometimes Perseus and Minerva). Use in a love letter: 'Fly to me on the talaria of your love, O my beloved!'

TAURIFOM *a.* Like a bull in shape. 'Ah, little Stephanie! Playing Mozart on the clavichord! And only nine years old! The experience would be perfect – if only she weren't so tauriform.'

TECHNOLATOR *n.* A person who is unduly worshipful of technology, gadgets, machinery and the like. Everyone knows at least one technolator. He will play interminably with your broken sewing machine, radiogram, carburettor, etc., *without ever fixing it.*

TELESTEREOSCOPE *n.* An optical instrument which delivers to the observer the image in relief of a distant object. Yes, this is the Superior Person's name for those 3-D glasses you get at the 3-D cinema. Use the term casually, and once only, for maximum effect.

TERRAQUEOUS *a.* Living both on land and in water. A surfie.

THANATOPHOBIA *n.* The morbid dread of death or dying. Ironic that it should be a *morbid* dread.

THEODICY *n.* A theological theory that asserts God's

justice in creating the world. (Despite all the evidence to the contrary, such as the existence of daytime television talks shows, Japanese drumming bands, etheric energy healing practitioners, etc., etc.)

THEOGONY *n.* The genealogy of a god or gods. For a pleasing effect of tapinosis (see under *trope*), refer to your sister-in-law's labours on the family genealogy as her 'ongoing theogony project'.

THERMESTHESIA *n.* Sensitivity to heat. Long, long ago, before most of us were born, the virtuoso violinist Jascha Heifetz gave his debut recital in New York. In the audience, sitting together, were the already eminent violinist Mischa Elman and the great pianist Leopold Godowsky. It was a warm night, and during the interval Elman took the opportunity to remove his jacket, saying to Godowsky: 'Don't you think it's rather hot in here tonight?' Replied Godowsky: 'Not for pianists.'

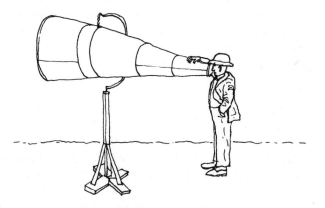

telestereoscope

THINNIFY *v.* To thin, or thin out. Do not be surprised by this seemingly otiose extension of a simple word so adequate in itself. Remember how *press*, as a verb, became *pressure*, and *pressure* became *pressurise*?

THURIBLE *n.* A censer, i.e., church vessel in which incense is ceremonially burnt. Superior Person's word for any device for the controlled inhalation of certain substances. A *thurifer* is the one who swings the censer during the ceremony. 'I'll just be down the backyard behind the shed with a few of my thurifer friends.'

TICKLER COIL *n.* A radio term. A tickler coil is a regenerative coil coupled in series with the plate circuit, used to intensify sound in a receiving circuit, through a feedback action. A true *technolater* (q.v.) might perhaps invite his beloved into his bedroom with an undertaking to show her his tickler coil.

TITTUP *v.* To frolic and generally kick up your heels, dancing or prancing along. A good word to introduce into your square-dance calls; but make sure to give equal emphasis to both syllables.

TOGGERY *n.* Collective noun for your togs, i.e., clothing. 'So – we're off to the beach and then on to the pictures. Everyone got their toggery?'

TOPECTOMY *n.* A surgical procedure in which the surgeon removes certain prefrontal cortical areas of the brain. 'Well, Rachel, I must say Shane looks absolutely wonderful since you've come back from overseas! He seems a new man! Tell me – did he have one of those Mexican topectomies?'

TOXICOPHOBIA *n.* The morbid dread of poison. The story is well known of the Roman emperor whose fear of being poisoned was so great that all his food was tasted before being passed to him. He succumbed when passed a dish of pre-tasted food so hot that it burnt his tongue, whereupon he called urgently for a drink of water. The poison was in the water. The moral: morbid dreads, useful though they are, do not necessarily protect you.

TRANSUBSTANTIATION *n.* Everyone is familiar with this term as signifying the transformation of bread and wine, during the Eucharist, into the body and blood respectively of Christ. A less well-known, but equally correct, meaning is a transformation of anything into something which is essentially different. Thus: 'Joel is actually wearing a tie to his graduation ceremony? And . . . what's this? Can it be? A suit? A suit *and* a tie? And he's shaved, actually shaved? I have seen it with my own eyes – a true transubstantiation!'

TRICHOTILLOMANIA *n.* A condition in which the sufferer frenziedly tears his hair. 'Look at it this way, Mr Birdworth; at least your baldness makes you immune to trichotillomania.'

TROPE *n.* The figurative use of a word, and hence something well represented in the illustrative examples given in this volume. Also, less correctly but commonly used to mean any figure of speech. In that sense of the word, the Superior Person should familiarise himself or herself with all of the following figures of speech, and drop them casually into conversation at a moment's notice:

· *anadiplosis* repetition of an end at the next beginning: 'Though I yield, I yield gladly.'

· *anastrophe* reversal of normal order: 'lexicographer supreme'.

· *asyndeton* omission of a conjunction between clauses: 'We loved, we laughed.'

· *brachylogia* omission of a conjunction between words or phrases: 'I have beauty, intelligence, wealth.'

· *diacope* repetition with a word between: 'goddess, beautiful goddess'.

· *epanados* repetition but in reverse order: 'Must we leave? Leave we must.'

· *epanalepsis* ending a group of words with the same word that began it. As in the title of a 1926 silent Our Gang short: *Uncle Tom's Uncle*.

· *epanorthosis* addition of a correction: 'I love you – no, I adore you.'

· *hendiadys* expressing an idea with two nouns: 'doom and gloom'.

· *hypallage* applying an adjective to the 'wrong' word: 'I had a sleepless night.'

· *litotes* affirming something by denying its negative: 'He's no slouch.'

· *metaplasmus* misspelling that still serves its purpose. See the signs on any fruit stall.

· *metonymy* substituting an attribute for the thing itself: 'I serve the crown.'

· *paradiastole* sarcastic euphuism as a means of disparagement, as in Ambrose Bierce's description of a monkey as being 'imperfectly beautiful'.

- *pleonasm* needless duplication of meaning: 'illustrating example'.
- *polysyndeton* a surfeit of conjunctions. See any Hemingway story.
- *praeteritio* drawing attention to something by claiming to ignore it: 'I will make no mention during this campaign of my opponent's criminal record.'
- *prosthesis* tacking letters on to the beginning of a word: 'bewail'.
- *syllepsis* relating the same word to two others in different senses: 'I swallowed my pride and an aspirin.'
- *synaloepha* combining two words with an omitted letter: 'shouldn't'.
- *synaesthesia* expressing one sensory experience by another: 'A heavy silence'.
- *synecdoche* substituting the part of the whole: 'ten head of cattle'.
- *tapinosis* belittling something or someone by sarcastic hyperbole: 'Well, here comes His Lordship!' (as your husband arrives on the scene).
- *zeugma* a verb governing two incongruous objects: 'She lost her heart and her purse.' (See also *syllepsis*.)

Why not have a 'Figure of Speech of the Month' for every month? Confound your friends with remarks such as 'I came, I saw, I conquered – ah yes – it's asyndeton month!'

In case the above brief guide to the world of the trope seems a little technical, let me assure you that a vastly more impenetrably esoteric field is that of prosody, which despite its name is not about the technicalities of prose but rather the technicalities of verse. Look into it at your peril.

TUBIFORM *a.* Shaped like a tube. 'OK, tonight's family conference has been called with one agenda item only. We need to decide which of Paige's two aspiring suitors should take her to the prom. Which is it to be – the tauriform or the tubiform?'

TUCK *n.* As is well known, this is now a verb meaning to insert, but in the sixteenth and seventeenth centuries a tuck was a type of short sword or dagger. 'Just let me slip a tuck in here between the ribs,' you might caringly whisper to your most over-dressed competitor at the ballroom-dancing championships.

TURGESCENCE *n.* Swelling or swollen; often with metaphorical connotations of pomposity. 'And now, it's that time of our meeting when we bow to the turgescence of our representative in the highest counsels of government. Ladies and gentlemen, I give you Senator ...'

TURRICULATE *a.* Topped by a turret, i.e., by a small ornamental tower of the kind sometimes seen on top of a building. Add it to your armoury of hairdo appraisal terminology.

TYPHLOSIS *n.* Blindness. 'And finally, I'd like to thank our long-suffering umpires and referees, who have given their time freely throughout the season to officiate at matches, week in, week out, often despite inconvenience – and even illness, as with Mr Middlebroom, whose recurring typhlosis is well known to us all and has not made things any easier for him. It is a thankless task, and must ever remain so – especially in his case.'

U

UBIQUITARIAN *n.* One whose existence is ubiquitous, i.e., who is everywhere. Said to be a characteristic of the God of pantheists, and for that matter of Christians; though somehow it does seem difficult to see the divine presence in the *Roseanne* show.

UDOMETER *n.* Another Superior Person's word for a rain gauge. (See also *pluviometer*.) If at all possible, use the two words in the one sentence.

ULTRAIST *n.* An extremist or radical in views or behaviour. 'I think you'll like Jackson, Dad: he's an absolute ultraist, just like you.'

ULUSCULE *n.* A little ulcer. When your academic acquaintance is showing off his technical expertise in bibliography by talking interminably about his majuscules and miniscules (which a normal person would call upper- and lower-case letters), you may find that you can suspend the flow of his expatiation with a passing reference to uluscules.

UMBRAGEOUS *a.* Shady or shaded; quick to take offence, irritable. A nice double meaning. 'You're so umbrageous, Leigh …'

UNCUS *n.* The hook with which the corpses of defeated gladiators were dragged out of the arena, or those of executed criminals from the *carnificina* (see *robur*). Suggested as a term for the hook on the end of a long pole with which music-hall performers whose acts were dying on stage were traditionally hauled off. 'Get out the uncus!' you arrange for everyone to cry in unison, halfway through the boss's speech at the office Christmas party.

UNGUENT *n.* An ointment or salve, originally for anointing though nowadays more commonly medicated for application as a *cerate* (q.v.). A good conversation-stopper at the dinner table: 'Can anyone tell me – exactly what is the difference between a cerate and an unguent?'

UNGUICULATE *a.* Equipped with hooks, nails and/or claws. 'So, Justin, you ask my advice as to whether you should marry Crystal. Well, she certainly has substantial investments and real property . . . but, let's look at it this way – she *is* unguiculate.'

UNGULIGRADE *a.* Walking on hoofs. As a horse, a cow, the great god Pan, etc. 'Great boat shoes, darling! Love the extra height those platforms give you! Now you're truly unguligrade!'

UNIVOCAL *a.* Having only one meaning; or, said of several people expressing themselves with one voice.

Rather ironic that a word which means 'having only one meaning' should itself have two.

URINIFEROUS *a.* Carryng urine. 'Behold, the uriniferous phial!' you cry triumphantly to your doctor as you emerge from the little room with your specimen.

URINOUS *a.* Looking like urine. One for the wine buffs. 'Ah yes, an excellent chardonnay, truly excellent! Medium-bodied . . . delightfully affectionate to the palate . . . not too fruity . . . lightly wooded . . . the cutest little varietal aroma . . . and urinous to a fault!'

URUSHIOL *n.* A poisonous, irritant fluid; the active element in poison ivy. Something you could profess to have put in the salad dressing, leaving the others to look it up later.

USTION *n.* The act of setting fire to something, or the state of being set fire to. From the Latin *ustus*, past participle of *urere*, to burn. Pronounced 'usch'n'. Always to be used in preference to its longer synonym *combustion*.

ustion

V

VASTATION *n.* Spiritual purification through the *ustion* (q.v.) of evil. 'Young man, be advised that I have performed vastation upon all those videotaped movies in your collection which have titles that include the word "blood" or the word "zombie".'

VATICINATE *v.* To foretell or prophesy. 'So tell me, darling, do your remarks about my employment prospects, now that I have been "let go", as the company so charmingly put it, constitute an act of true vaticination, or merely an attempt to add that extra edge to my dysphoria?'

VELAMEN *n.* A veil worn by women, concealing the whole body as well as the head. 'Have you thought of wearing a velamen to the ball, Mrs Underdown? It would really make you look your best, dear.'

VERBIGERATE *v.* To speak repetitively in totally meaningless language. A symptom of certain types of mental illness. And of readers who take this book too seriously.

VERTUGADE *n.* A farthingale, i.e., a circular whalebone frame fastened around the hips – in former times a piece of women's underwear designed to provide a basis for extending the petticoat. Once tied around the waist it was impossible for the wearer to lower her arms, which she was therefore obliged to rest on the vertugade as if on a shelf. In England sometimes irreverently called a 'bum-roll'. Claimed by Rabelais to have been invented in a Spanish brothel for erotic purposes.

VIBRATIUNCULATION *n.* A slight shudder or vibration. As you stand beside the mechanic leaning over the engine of your car, you might say, 'It's just a little vibratiunculation, for want of a better word, that I get sometimes when starting on a hill.' Don't expect a reaction, though; he won't be paying any attention to anything you say anyway.

VICISSITUDINARY *a.* Subject to constant change. 'Sorry, Brad – Simone's out with Owen tonight. And I think it's Craig tomorrow night. She's going through one of her vicissitudinary phases at the moment. Hang in there, man.'

VIGESIMAL *a.* Pertaining to the number twenty. 'As we all gather here to celebrate Daniel's twenty-first, it is chastening to remember that only a year ago this young man was – how can I express this without embarrassing him – vigesimate.'

VIRGATE *a.* Long, slender and straight. 'I'm bringing Celine over tonight, Dad, and I do not wish to hear the word "virgate" at any time during the evening – is that clear?'

VITELLINE *a.* To do with egg yolk. 'Ah, a truly vitelline restorative!' you exclaim, as you scoff your eggnog, the morning after.

VITRESCIBLE *a.* Having the quality of forming a viscous, glassy layer when subjected to heat. Another suitable term for hairdo appraisal.

VIVANDIÈRE *n.* In former times, a woman who supplied food and drink to soldiers in the field. 'Ah, our vivandière cometh!' you cry, as your wife emerges from the kitchen with salad and punch for your backyard barbecue.

VOLE *n.* A kind of mouse. Alternatively, the winning of all the tricks in a deal when playing the card game *écarté* – hence the expression *to go the vole*, i.e., to risk everything in the hope of a big win. 'I'm going the vole on this one!' you cry, as you release the pet mice from their cage during your wife's bridge party.

VORLAGE *n.* A skiing term, vorlage being a stance in which the skier leans forward at an angle of less than a right angle to the line of ground surface. "Hmm, he's in vorlage tonight,' you say, as the returning *pater familias* is observed approaching the front door, his tenuous maintenance of an angle from the perpendicular bespeaking a longer than usual stopover at Joe's Bar on the way home.

VORTIGINOUS *a.* Moving as if caught in a vortex, i.e., rotating towards a notional central point. Mode of locomotion of one suffering from the effects of *porsonian* (q.v.) *potomania* (q.v.).

VRIL *n.* A *neoterism* (q.v.) of ninenteenth-century author Edward Bulwer-Lytton, denoting a force of psychic vibrational energy of colossal destructive power. Seen by some of his modern readers as an inspired forecast of nuclear energy, but now thought to be a reference to premenstrual tension.

VULNERARY *a.* or *n.* Having a curative effect on wounds. 'A little vulnerary unguent for your shaving cuts, darling?'

VULPICIDE *n.* The killing of a fox *other than by hunting with hounds*; or one who does that. The italics are mine. A puzzling one indeed. This is the meaning of the term as given by both Webster and Oxford. Yet why should hunting with hounds be excluded from the definition? The implication would seem to be that there is a moral bonus, so to speak, in hunting with hounds; that this is an *ethical* way to despatch the wily Reynard, and that other methods are unethical. Yet what other methods are there? In what circumstances could the word vulpicide actually be used? 'I say, old chap – passed a fox on the way across the meadow this morning – got him on the head with a four iron!' 'You absolute rotter! You could have got out a few hounds and had them tear his throat out; but oh no, you just had to commit vulpicide!'

W

WADSET *n.* A Scottish legal term, a wadset being a pledge of some piece of property as security for a loan. A wadsetter is the one giving the loan and receiving the wadset. 'Be thou my wadsetter until payday, in recognition of which I leave with thee my entire collection of Scottish country-dance music CDs.'

Wafter

WAFTER *n.* A person who wafts, that is to say, floats gently along. *Wafture* is that which is wafted, as for example an odour. 'Hmm, the distinct fragrance of

Athol's aftershave. Such a wafture surely precedes the wafter himself. Be ready to open the window.'

WARISON *n.* One of those curious and useful words which have two meanings that are so different as to be all but diametrically opposed. In this case: a signal for attack; and a reward or other form of benign gift. 'You deserve a warison from me, Courtney; it shall come when you least expect it.'

WATTLE *n.* A fowl's jollop. But what, I hear you ask, is a jollop? A jollop is a wrinkled, brightly coloured strip of flesh hanging from the throat. When Dylan emerges from his daily preening hour in the bathroom, you peer at his face and then ask, with a hint of concern in your voice, 'Don't think me rude, but … is that a wattle growing on your left cheek?'

WEEN *v.* To suppose or think (that something is the case). Archaic terms beginning with *w* have a special charm, and should be used remorselessly. See *welkin* and *wistless*. Use all three in the one sentence if you can. (Do not write to the author telling him how you did this.)

WELKIN *n.* Archaic term for the sky, especially in the grand sense of the great vault of the heavens above. 'Ah, truly a wonderful welkin today, I ween.'

WHIFFLE *n.* An unimportant person; someone more pretentious than significant. In short, a whippersnapper, i.e., a whipsnapper, a cracker of whips – someone who makes a lot of noise to no purpose.

WILLIWAW *n.* A sudden and powerful downdraught of wind moving violently down the slope of a mountainous coast. You could so characterise your father's post-prandial snores as he reclines, comatose, in his armchair before the television.

WISTLESS *a.* Slow to notice, not observant, inattentive. 'A little wistless tonight, I *ween* [q.v.], dearest?' (When he has not noticed your new hairstyle.)

wistless

WOODIE *n.* Scottish humorous term for the gallows or the hangman's rope. Ah, those good old Scottish hangman's jokes – you don't hear many of them these days, do you?

WRAPRASCAL *n.* A long, loose overcoat in common use in the eighteenth century. Today, Superior Person's word for the trench coat.

X

XANTHIC *a.* Yellow in colour. 'Oh, Jessica dear,' you say, as you inspect the toilet bowl; 'been OD'ing on Mummy's multi-vitamin tablets again, have you?'

XENIAL *a.* To do with hospitality. 'And now, our genial host – I should say our genial xenial, I suppose …'

XENOGLOSSIA *n.* The supposed ability to communicate with others in a language which you do not know. (A term from the world of so-called 'psychic research'.) The impracticability of this concept is soon exposed if you attempt to talk with your teenager using some of the terms that you have heard him use in conversation with his friends. This will, however, at least afford him considerable entertainment, and you will be pressed, with much sniggering, to 'say that again' – something that he will never otherwise say to you.

XERIC *a.* Extremely dry. The metaphoric use is suggested. 'How droll, Gregor, how perfectly xeric your sense of humour is.' Pressed for an explanation, you make an offhand remark along the lines of 'From the Greek – you know – xerox, xeromorphy, xerophthalmia and all that – you know …'

XYSTUS *n.* An ancient Roman word, meaning the covered space in which athletes went through their physical preparations. The baths at Rome were furnished with large *xysti*, in which young men went through a number of exercises. A pleasingly archaic word for that feature of modern society, the gym.

Y

YATAGHAN *n.* A special form of Turkish scimitar in which the cutting edge of the blade has not one but two curves, one being convex and the other concave. 'Ah, Madam's taste in Persian carpets is beyond praise! As are Madam's skills in the ancient eastern art of price negotiation! Never before have I met a customer so eloquent, so persistent, so demanding of satisfaction! The many hours we have spent discussing the price and measurement of every carpet and every rug in my humble store are of inestimable value for me! As for this last difference of opinion between us on the price of this, my cheapest, smallest and most inferior rug – I could resolve it all now with one stroke of the yataghan – if Madam will permit?'

YEAN *v.* To bring forth young. (As, for example, sheep or goats – a term from the world of animal husbandry.) But don't tell the ambulance people over the phone that your wife is yeaning; they may not have read the book.

YGDRASIL *n.* The gigantic ash tree which, according to Norse mythology, binds together with its roots and branches the whole of earth, heaven and hell. Suggested as a pet name for that tree in your backyard – the one you want your husband to chop down before its spreading canopy brings total darkness to your clothesline, your herb garden and your sunbathing spot.

Z

ZARF *n.* A filigree metal holder for a hot coffee cup or glass. From the Arabic. One of those things they give you in coffee lounges to hold your steaming caffe-latte in. But why on earth are they made of metal, which is after all such an effective conductor of heat? 'Excuse me, miss; I've just burnt my fingers on my wife's zarf – could I possibly have a vulnerary unguent?'

ZEDOARY *n.* A type of turmeric root that has the medicinal function of strengthening the activity of the stomach. 'OK, everyone ready to order? We'll have six big burgers, five caramel sundaes, thirteen hash browns, five hot chocolates, eight medium french fries, seven blueberry muffins . . . and zedoaries all round, please.'

ZIGGURAT *n.* In ancient times, a Babylonian temple with stepped terraces giving it a pyramidal shape, so that each storey was a little smaller than the one below it. 'So, how's the party fare coming along? Ah, gingerbread men, chocolates crackles, yes, doughnuts with pink icing . . . and do I see one of your mother's ziggurat cakes in the making?'

ZOIC *a.* To do with animals or with the life of animals. 'Yes, it's an interesting place to live. I think you'll like it after you've settled in. The atmosphere's very laid back. The neighbours are very friendly. They don't stand on ceremony; they'll pop in to see you all the time – and you'll find them truly zoic.'

ZONA *n.* In ancient times, a girdle that was used to gird up the skirts of a dress, in the interests of freedom of action. On solemn occasions the girdle was relaxed, so that the folds of the dress would hang down to the feet. During a marriage ceremony it was taken off altogether. 'Any chance of doffing the old zona tonight, babe?' might be a novel way of approaching an old subject.

ZOOPHILOUS *a.* Animal-loving – a practice illegal in some countries. (Pray forgive the lexicographer his little facetiae – especially towards the end of the 'z's'.)

ZOOPHOBIA *n.* Morbid dread of animals. Could perhaps be applied to vegetarians across the dinner table ('No spare ribs, Kylie? I didn't know you were zoophobic'), though at the risk of a truly xeric comeback, since vegetarians' hunger for solid matter will certainly have led them to a reading of this book.

ZYGOSIS *n.* The conjugation, or joining together, of two sex cells. Convince the shy couple that when they sit down with the priest to discuss the wedding ceremony they should check that the zygosis occurs straight after the signing of vows.

Sources

The sources from which the words are derived include, as would be expected, various editions of the better-known dictionaries (more especially, Oxford, Webster's, Chambers, and Funk & Wagnalls) and also the following specific works:

Bombaugh, C. C. *Oddities and Curiosities of Words and Literature*. Dover, N.Y., 1961.

Byrne, Josefa Heifetz. *Mrs Byrne's Dictionary of Unusual, Obscure and Preposterous Words*. Citadel Press, Secaucus, N.J., 1976.

Drever, James. *A Dictionary of Psychology*. Penguin, London, 1958.

Haubrich, William S. *Medical Meanings: A Glossary of Word Origins*. Harcourt Brace Jovanovich, San Diego, 1984.

Hill, Robert H. (comp.). *A Dictionary of Difficult Words*. Signet, N.Y., 1975.

Johnson, Samuel. *A Dictionary of the English Language. Abstracted from the Folio Edition by the Author*. Allison et al., London, 1824.

Kupper, W. H. *Dictionary of Psychiatry and Psychology*. Colt Press, N.J., 1953.

Ogilvie, John (ed.). *A Supplement to the Imperial Dictionary: English, Technical and Scientific*. Blackie and Son, Glasgow, 1855.

Riley, P. A., and Cunningham, P. J. *The Faber Pocket Medical Dictionary*. Faber & Faber, London, 1977.

Shipley, Joseph T. *Dictionary of Word Origins*. Philosophical Library, N.Y., 1945.

The Family Bible Dictionary. Avenel Books, N.Y., n.d.

Tweney, C. F., and Hughes, L. E. C. (eds). *Chambers Technical Dictionary*, Macmillan, N.Y., 1965.

Urdang, Laurence (ed.). *The New York Times Everyday Reader's Dictionary of Misunderstood, Misused, Mispronounced Words*. Weathervane Books, N.Y., n.d.

Uvarov, E. B., and Chapman, D. R. *A Dictionary of Science*. Penguin, London, 1951.

Weekley, Ernest. *An Etymological Dictionary of Modern English*. Dover, N.Y., 1967.

A NOTE ON THE TYPE

The text of this book is set in Linotype Sabon, named after the type founder, Jacques Sabon. It was designed by Jan Tschichold and jointly developed by Linotype, Monotype and Stempel, in response to a need for a typeface to be available in identical form for mechanical hot metal composition and hand composition using foundry type.

Tschichold based his design for Sabon on a fount engraved by Garamond, and Sabon italic on a fount by Granjon. It was first used in 1966 and has proved and enduring modern classic.